STEVEN EHRLICH ARCHITECTS

A DYNAMIC SERENITY

MICHAEL WEBB

This book is dedicated to my loving mom, Betty Ehrlich, 1921-2000.

STEVEN EHRLICH ARCHITECTS

A DYNAMIC SERENITY

MICHAEL WEBB

First published in Australia in 2002 by
The Images Publishing Group Pty Ltd
ABN 89 059 734 431
6 Bastow Place, Mulgrave, Victoria, 3170, Australia
Telephone: +61 3 9561 5544 Facsimile: +61 3 9561 4860
Email: books@images.com.au
Website: www.imagespublishinggroup.com

Copyright © The Images Publishing Group Pty Ltd
The Images Publishing Group Reference Number: 372

National Library of Australia
Cataloguing-in-Publication data

Webb, Michael, 1937- .
A dynamic Serenity: Steven Ehrlich Architects.

Bibliography.
ISBN 1 86470 102 1.

1. Ehrlich, Steven, 1946- – Career in architecture. 2.
Architect-designed houses – California, Southern –
Pictorial works. 3. Architecture, Domestic – California,
Southern – 20th century – Pictorial works. I. Title.
(Series: House design; no. 3).

728.097949

Concept design and final art by The Graphic Image Studio
Film by Mission Productions
Printed by Paramount Printing Company Limited Hong Kong.

IMAGES has included on its website a page for special notices in relation
to this and its other publications.
Please visit: www.imagespublishinggroup.com

PREFACE

Designing houses has been one of my most fulfilling personal experiences. Houses dominated the first decade of my practice and remain an essential part of my work. I have always relished the opportunity to discover and celebrate the uniqueness of each client and site, even as my design approach has remained consistent: that simplicity and clarity are the best guides. Although some of my designs are complex, I proceed from straightforward architectural concepts.

It was in Africa that I learned much of what I have come to believe about houses. During a six-year post-university African sojourn practicing, teaching and observing architecture, I admired the clarity of purpose embodied in the continent's "architecture without architects." African dwellings are simple, direct and sustainable. They respond to the local climate and tread lightly on the earth. My travels in Africa, as well as Latin America and Asia, have imbued in me an appreciation for indigenous traditions that I term "architectural anthropology."

As an architect living and working in Southern California, I obviously face a whole different set of circumstances and challenges than African builders. Viewed from an airplane, the grid of Los Angeles' streets and freeways stretches like a giant computer chip to the horizon. The resemblance is not only figurative: Los Angeles is a digital-age mecca, strongly oriented toward the future. The city's nearly limitless ability to respond instantly to new information makes it an incubator of change. My work has absorbed and reflects the city's fast-paced, kinetic spirit.

My houses are part of the lineage of Californian modernism as pioneered by the residential work of Richard Neutra and Rudolph Schindler, who maximized enjoyment of our sublime climate by eliminating the barrier between indoors and out. My work marries modernism with "global regionalism," an approach to design that is sensitive to local traditions, ethnicities and environment, while fully taking advantage of new technologies. Recently I have become enchanted by the possibilities of trans-formations in form and space. Through moving parts, simple and minimal places can morph into a multiplicity of environments. A room can be opened up to outdoor light and air or sealed off for privacy in response to changes in the time of day, season, or one's mood. Technology serves flexibility and versatility. Materials and design create livable and harmonious spaces rather than overcome the environment with technological "muscle."

Buildings, after all, exist to serve people. It is at home that we reconnect with nature, each other, and ourselves. As the world grows smaller and the pace of our lives quickens, it is more important than ever that the house becomes a place of refuge, a serene environment to replenish the soul.

My belief in the higher purpose of architecture, to bring people together in a place of beauty, guides my continuing journey.

Steven Ehrlich, Venice, California 2002

CONTENTS

8

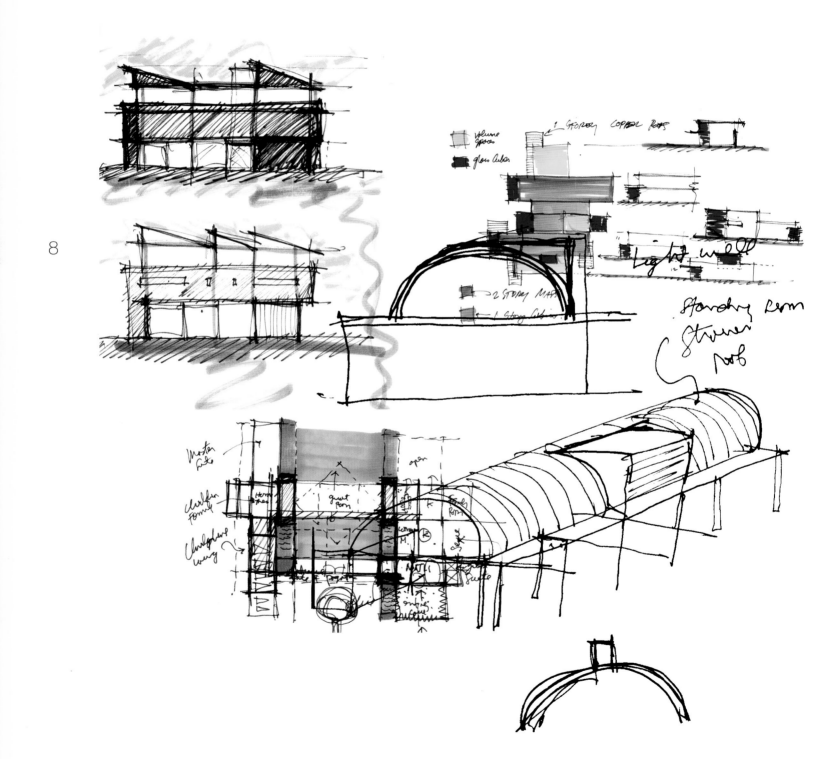

INTRODUCTION

In his two decades of practice in Los Angeles, Steven Ehrlich has won acclaim for master plans and commercial remodels, artists' studios, schools, colleges, libraries, retail, and offices—all distinguished by a consistency of thought and a diversity of expression. As if this were not enough for an atelier of 30 people, he has planned, built or remodeled more than 50 houses—most recently with principal James Schmidt—and for him, as for so many of his peers, they are the most rewarding of jobs. "There's a lot of emotion involved in their design, but it's worth it for the payback," he says. "Each is unique to the site and the owner—with whom you can enjoy a very personal engagement."

Good clients decide what they want, choose architects who listen carefully to their requests and have an intuitive grasp of what is not said, then leave them to find the best way to interpret that complex interplay of practical needs and private emotions. Ehrlich has been blessed with clients who appreciate his skill and sensitivity, and who encourage him to reach beyond the places he has been before. His houses are quiet, intelligent expressions of timeless principles and modern thinking that respond to site, climate, and context. Each is a variation on a theme that he—and architects he admires—has explored before, and a step forward. They draw on his experience of different cultures and the basic lessons of what works and what doesn't. "If you don't go to the next step you repeat yourself, but you don't want to cut loose and lose touch with who you are," he explains.

This book shows how he has balanced continuity and innovation in 11 projects that were completed or begun in the past decade. Each of the three groupings represents a different theme: designing for narrow urban sites in the Venice district of Los Angeles; remodeling and extending existing houses; and creating boldly articulated residences that expand into the landscape. Together, they demonstrate how simple ideas can enrich everyday living, delighting owners and all who experience them.

SELECTED WORKS

EHRLICH HOUSE

An architect's own house can be a declaration of principles pitched to like-minded clients or a modest shelter that serves as a retreat for family and friends. The residence that Ehrlich designed for himself in the oceanfront community of Venice is a bit of both. It is a reminder of where he began his practice in 1979 (in a remodeled Craftsman house now owned by another adventurous architect), and an expression of the ideas he has been developing ever since. Leaner and more compressed than the hillside house he built for his family in Santa Monica Canyon 12 years ago, it shows how one can make the most from the least on a skinny site with streets and a service alley on three sides and within a tight zoning envelope. Another challenge was to achieve a sense of richness and harmony on a tight budget as the architect tries to do with his schools and warehouses. The house fuses indoors and out, and makes good use of every level surface from courtyard to terraces. Ehrlich describes it as a "gathering place, where friends can drop by and hang out, and a pocket of tranquility to nourish the soul."

That mix of sociability and spirituality infuses everything that Ehrlich does, as he draws on his experience of living and working in Morocco, Nigeria and Japan, and on the intensity of his feelings for Southern California, where most of his work is located. All architects travel in search of inspiration, usually to Europe, sketchbook or camera in hand. Ehrlich went further and took longer, immersing himself for years in the culture of the countries he explored—as a Peace Corps volunteer in Africa and, later, in Japan when he was commissioned to build a showroom in Tokyo. As a result, his architecture incorporates, not merely the surfaces, but the underlying philosophy of what he saw and felt. In his public and private buildings there is a recurring emphasis on courtyards and outdoor living as a way of fostering communal interaction and creating peaceful environments that put one in touch with nature. The simplicity of his houses is animated by shifts of level and the juxtaposition of rough and refined materials, by natural ventilation and the magical play of light.

All of those qualities have a special relevance to the benign climate and casual lifestyle of Los Angeles as R.M. Schindler discovered 70 years ago. Schindler is the 'genius loci' for progressive LA architects, an inexhaustible source of ideas and details, and Ehrlich has absorbed some of these into his own work. The home he is designing for his family has affinities to the Lovell Beach House of 1926—in its verticality, the shift from mass at the rear to openness at the front, and the dramatic contrast between the lofty living area and low-ceilinged sleeping galleries.

There are also major differences: Schindler raised his living areas a story above the sand on a massive concrete frame and boldly expressed this on the long street façade; Ehrlich's wood-frame structure hugs the ground and a bamboo hedge screens its two open façades from the street. The expressiveness comes from the contrast between rough and smooth surfaces. A textured concrete stucco wall with narrow openings shields the house from another residence to the east and provides a backdrop for art. Other solid walls are faced with self-

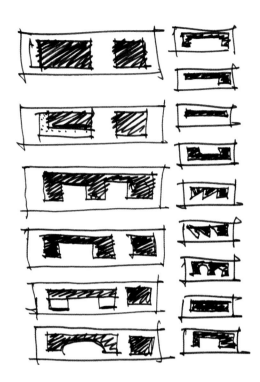

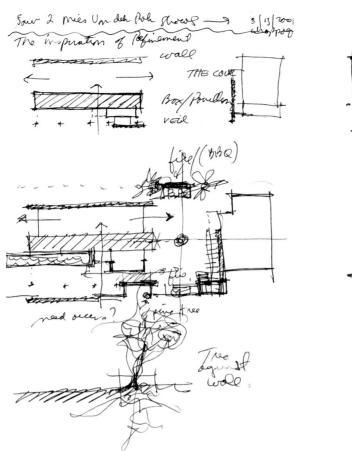

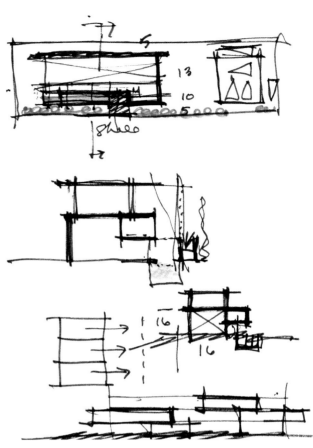

rusting steel, and pull-down blinds on a skeletal steel frame block the western sun. Stairs lead up to a pair of mezzanine-level sleeping lofts; a glass bridge spans the living room to another flight that leads up to the second floor master suite and study, with decks tucked under the steel frame at both levels. A section of the monopitch roof tips up to serve as a linear skylight.

A strong Japanese influence pervades the house. The narrow courtyard evokes a landscape, especially when the blinds are drawn and the bamboo hedge casts moving shadows on the white scrim. A rectangle of plywood set into the floor of the living area can be raised to allow diners to sit on the edge of the void and eat at eye level with the pool. The outdoors is as much a part of the house as the open-plan interior.

Energy conservation is a major concern. The 15-foot-high living/dining room opens up on three sides through pocketing glass doors to the north, glass sliders to the lap pool that is tucked under the steel frame, and through pivoting steel doors to the yard and the detached studio/guest bedroom at the south end of the site. In this mode it becomes an airy shelter, naturally ventilated by ocean breezes, and requiring no air conditioning. The concrete slab absorbs the sun's warmth in winter, and photovoltaic cells may contribute to the underfloor heating.

The architect's goal is to live in harmony with nature and with the community, which has long attracted artists and other free spirits, and is one of the few neighborhoods in the metropolis where people casually stroll a few blocks to call on friends. This is the eighth house he has designed in Venice and the latest in a series, all of which respond to narrow plots, the funky urbanism of what was formerly a bohemian slum, and a freedom to build whatever you want within the mandatory limits on height and setback.

Venice has an edgy, alive character; galleries, restaurants and clubs are thriving, and it's conveniently close to the beach—the one great open space that everyone can use. However, gentrification is proceeding apace, and, as prices soar, clapboard cottages are being replaced by blocks whose builders exploit every loophole in the regulations to max out the sites.

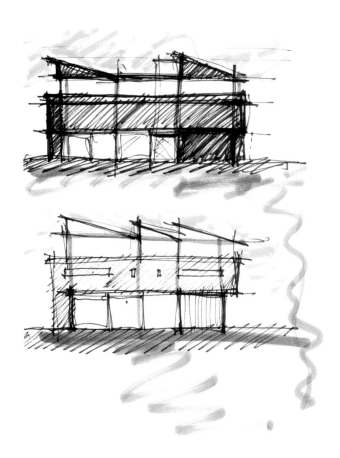

Ehrlich's strategy is to carve away the box, allowing the open and enclosed areas to flow into each other, blurring boundaries and fostering the illusion of spaciousness. He speaks of creating "transformative environments," in which an interior can be opened or closed at the touch of a button, making it habitable in every kind of weather and thus doubling its utility. Shifts from confined to lofty volumes and movement through a space can heighten owners' sensitivity to their living environments, so that they value them more for their visceral quality than their square footage. All of this is a healthy corrective to the American cult of gigantism.

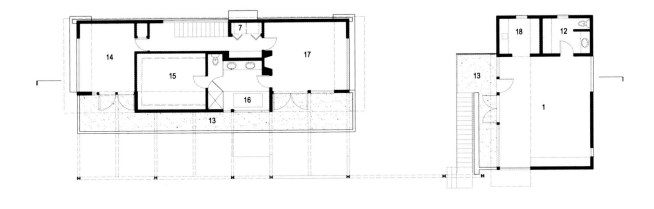

16

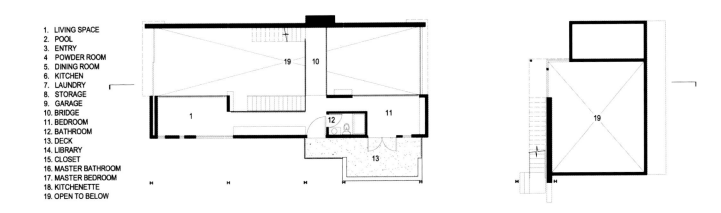

1. LIVING SPACE
2. POOL
3. ENTRY
4 POWDER ROOM
5. DINING ROOM
6. KITCHEN
7. LAUNDRY
8. STORAGE
9. GARAGE
10. BRIDGE
11. BEDROOM
12. BATHROOM
13. DECK
14. LIBRARY
15. CLOSET
16. MASTER BATHROOM
17. MASTER BEDROOM
18. KITCHENETTE
19. OPEN TO BELOW

MEZZANINE PLAN

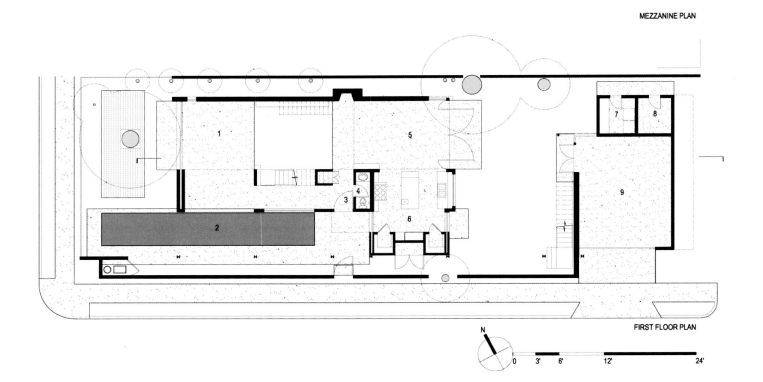

N

0   3'   6'   12'   24'

FIRST FLOOR PLAN

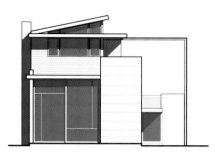

WEST ELEVATION

EAST ELEVATION

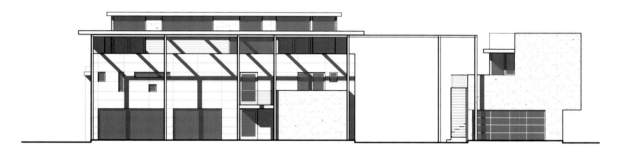

SOUTH ELEVATION

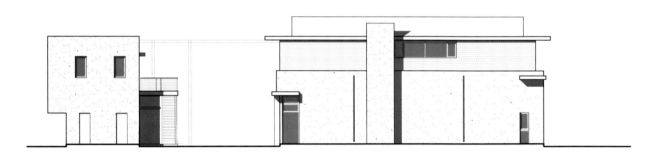

NORTH ELEVATION

SECTION

0   3'   6'   12'   24'

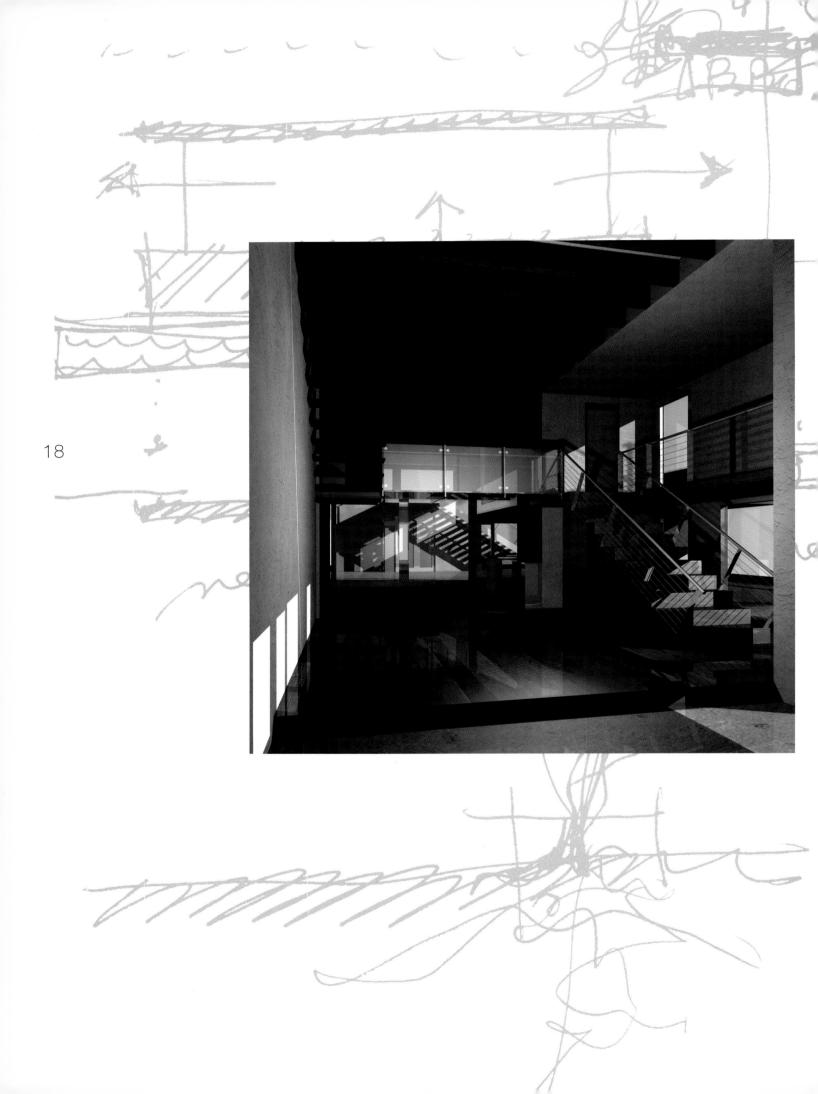

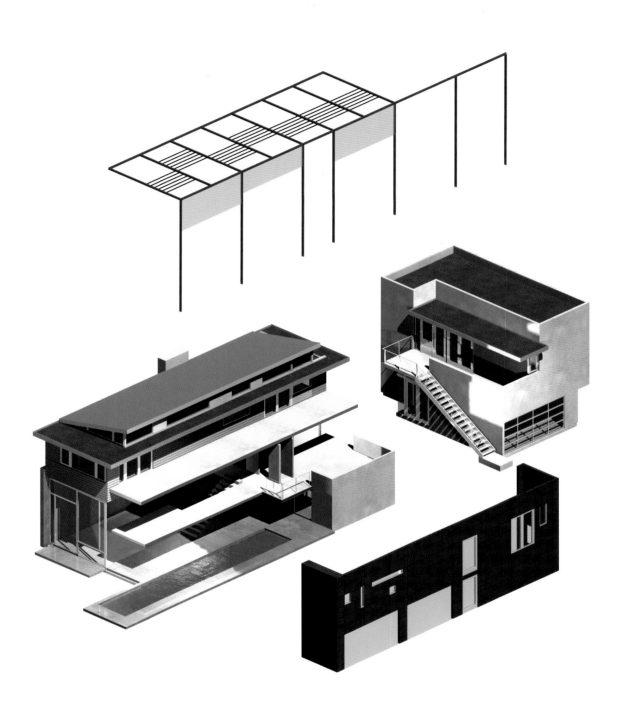

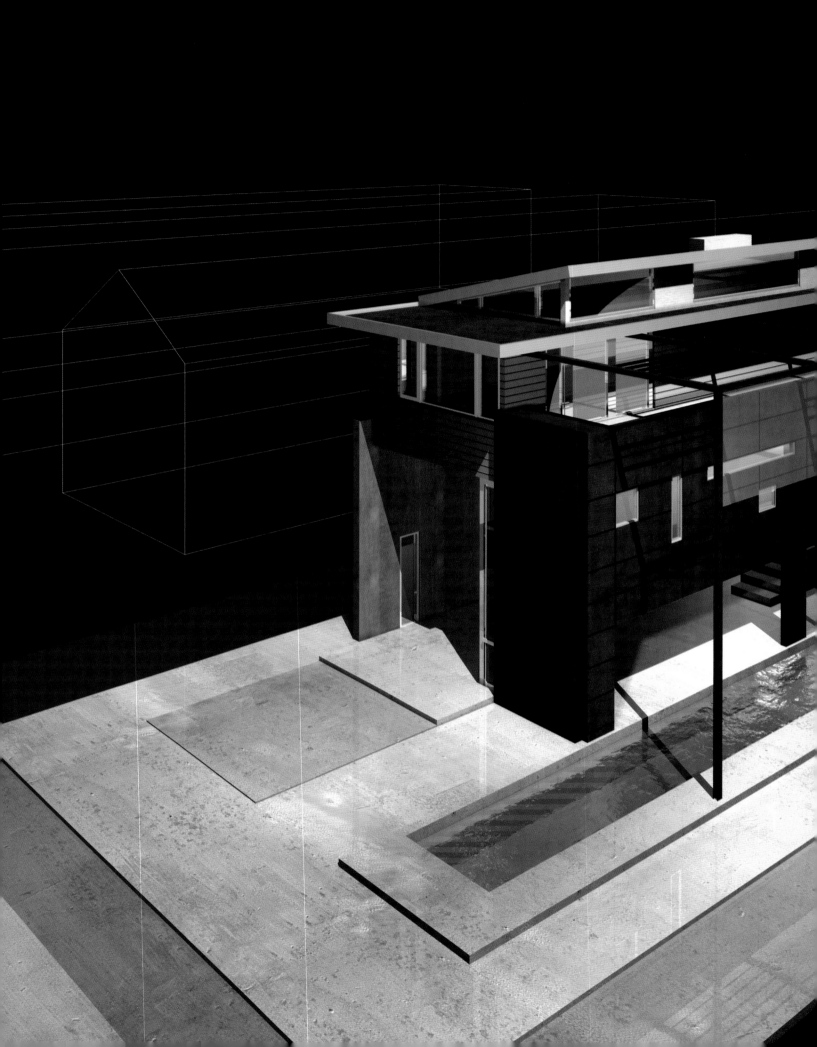

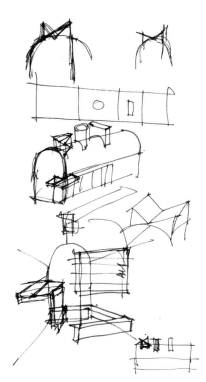

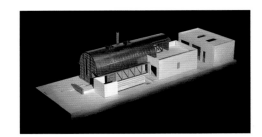

FARRELL HOUSE

Many of the ideas that Ehrlich has developed for himself were earlier explored in the Venice house he designed for Perry Farrell. A progressive rock musician who spends much of his life in planes, hotel rooms and concert shells, and performing, recording and producing Lollapalooza and other innovative festivals, Farrell wanted a place of repose, where he could relax with friends and go surfing. Himself a former nomad, Ehrlich had an intuitive understanding of his client's need for grounding and purification, and won immediate approval for a design that abstracts traditional notions of house and garden. The street façade of the Farrell house is enigmatic: an arched expanse of black plywood overlaid with a grid of battens, broken only by a projecting panel of colored glass, a recessed door, and an asymmetrical red wood-strip cross which turns back along the side gutters, like a ribbon tied around an odd-shaped parcel. Slate pavers cross a tangled lawn; to the right of the entrance is a low purple wall, topped by a red trellis.

Beyond the black wall, Ehrlich constructed what he describes as a basilica with a rounded vault, sitting atop the raised foundation of the cottage that formerly occupied the site, with a lap pool running down the side. He also retained a rear bedroom, which now serves guests, but everything else is new and is unified by a strong central axis terminating in a detached garage that mimics the profile of the house and doubles as a sculpture studio. The great room that occupies the front half of the house opens to the pool through pocketing glass sliders and this doubles its size since the walled court serves as an outdoor living room. The interior is treated as a single space, with a tiled kitchen and an Asian-style table rising from a maple platform, leading to a sitting area around the hearth and the open-ended mezzanine sleeping gallery.

The volumetric simplicity is enriched by a strong sense of materiality. Red trim sets off the standing-seam metal roof and toned stucco. Front and side doors are of galvanized metal; inner doors are veiled with panels of diaphanous silk, photo-printed with nude figures, which waft in the breeze. The vault is lined with curved panels of maple-veneered plywood, which is also used for shelves and cabinets, accented with the darker tone of paduck. Blue and yellow tiles highlight the smooth concrete around the pool and the terrazzo-patterned linoleum within. Tough, sensual, and restrained, the house is an urban oasis that captures the free spirit of Venice even though it is shut off from its neighbors.

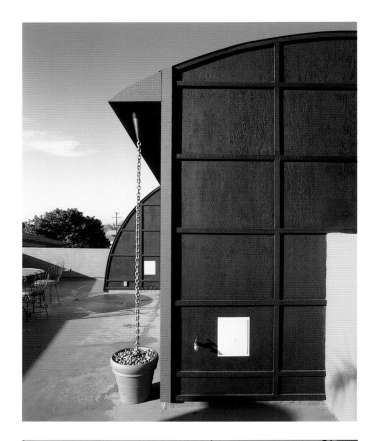

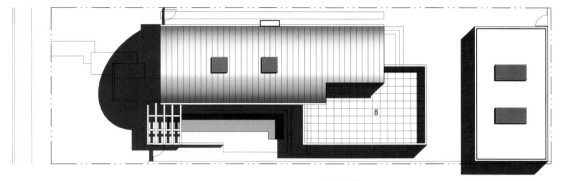

ROOF PLAN

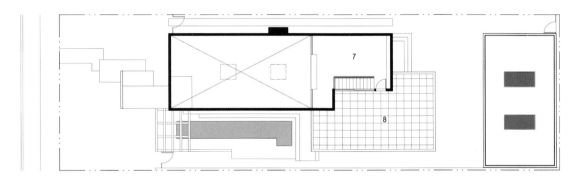

SECOND FLOOR PLAN

1. KITCHEN
2. DINING AREA
3. LIVING ROOM
4. BEDROOM
5. MASTER BATH
6. STUDIO
7. LOFT
8. ROOF DECK

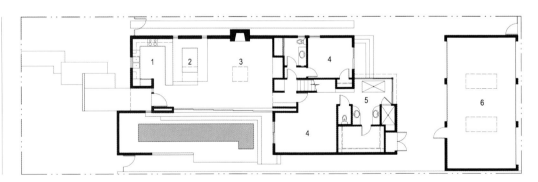

FIRST FLOOR PLAN

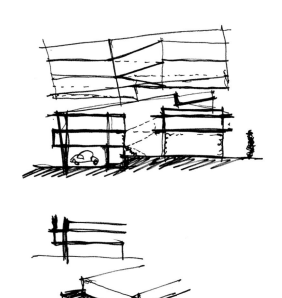

WEBSTER HOUSE

A house that Ehrlich and Schmidt designed for a young Australian couple also responds to a tightly confined site. The narrow rectangular plot extends from a walk street on the south side, dropping five feet to a service alley on the north. That shift in grade allowed the architects to accommodate a garage under two multi-purpose levels while staying within the height limit. The studios to the rear are linked to the living area and upper-level master suite on the walk street by a stepped-section service spine along the east side, and an interior courtyard with a reflecting pool to the west. Steel I-beams frame roll-up garage doors on the front block, creating an open axis that extends through the living area, across the courtyard, up a flight of steps and into the rear studio through another roll-up door.

"Enclosed spaces can become porous and open," says Ehrlich. "It's all about making more of less." The easy flow of space is enhanced by the use of steel grilles for stair treads and galleries that seem to float in the lofty void at the center of the house, bathed in light from above and leading up to a roof terrace that's fully equipped for parties. Looking over the neighboring roofs to ocean and mountains, one realizes that the house is like a flower that has pushed up from its dark slot of space in search of the sun. And yet, for all its feeling of openness it is largely concealed from public view.

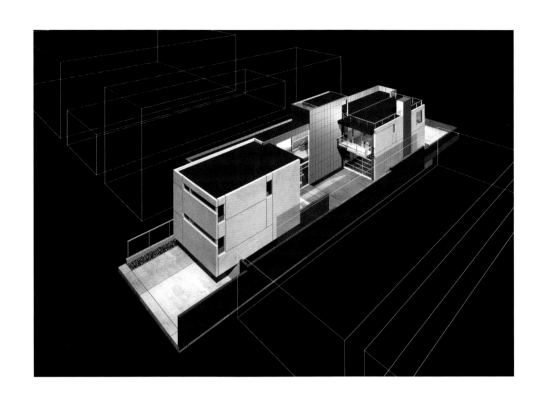

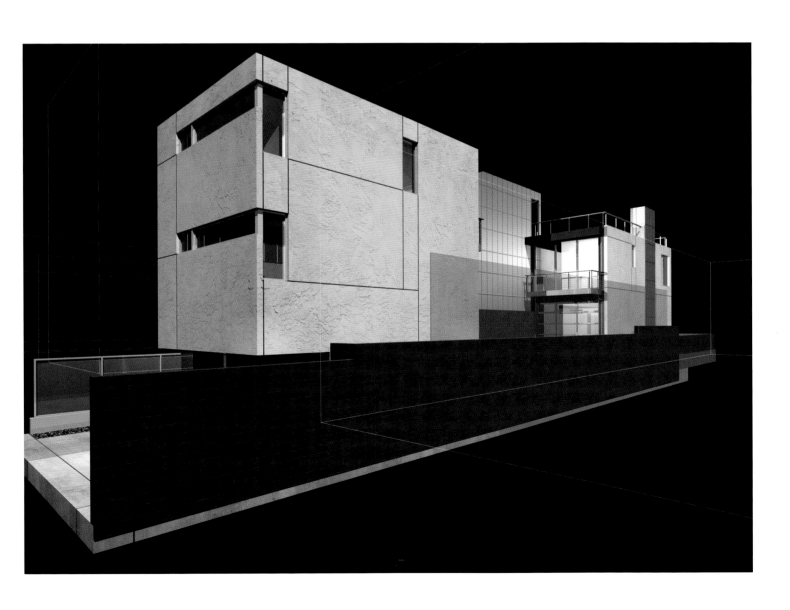

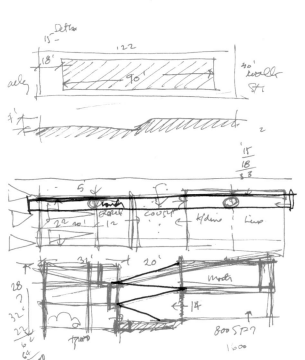

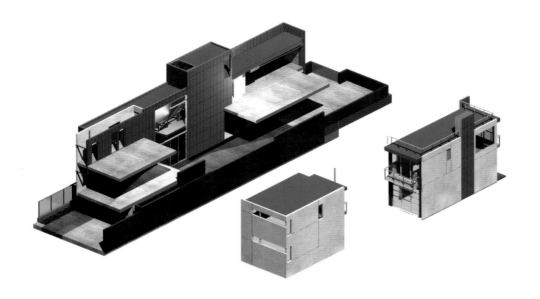

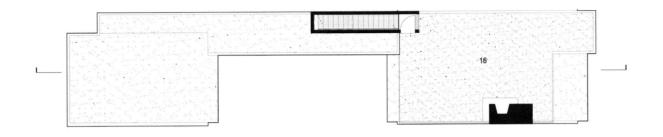

ROOF PLAN

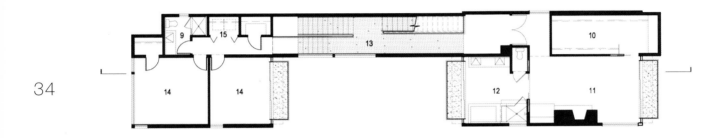

34

SECOND FLOOR PLAN

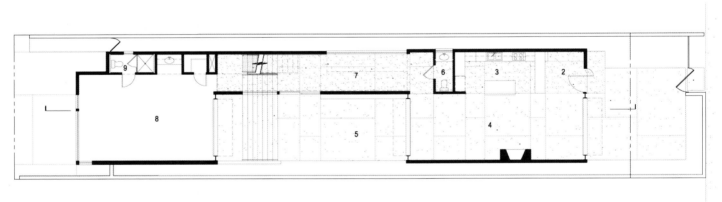

FIRST FLOOR PLAN

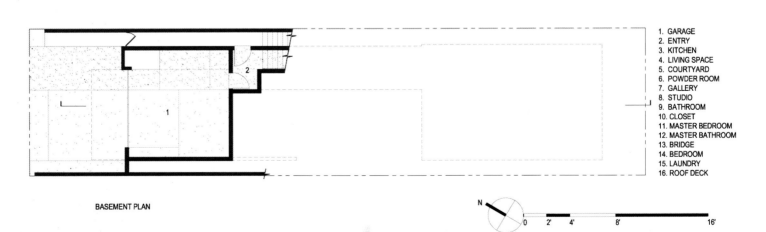

BASEMENT PLAN

1. GARAGE
2. ENTRY
3. KITCHEN
4. LIVING SPACE
5. COURTYARD
6. POWDER ROOM
7. GALLERY
8. STUDIO
9. BATHROOM
10. CLOSET
11. MASTER BEDROOM
12. MASTER BATHROOM
13. BRIDGE
14. BEDROOM
15. LAUNDRY
16. ROOF DECK

N

0   2'   4'   8'   16'

EAST ELEVATION

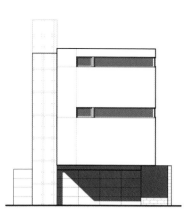

WEST ELEVATION

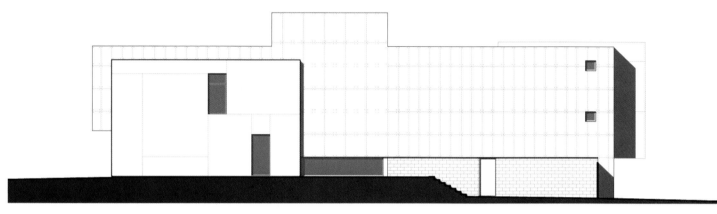

NORTH ELEVATION

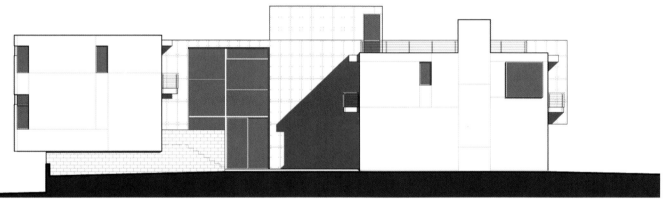

SOUTH ELEVATION

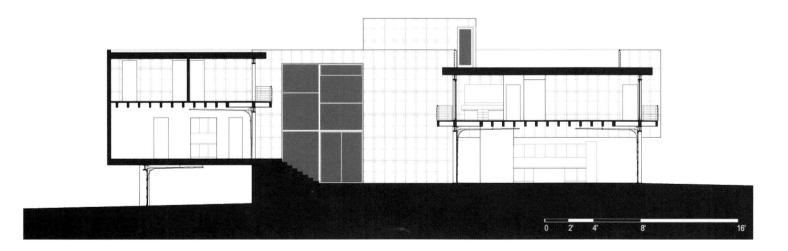

0   2'   4'   8'   16'

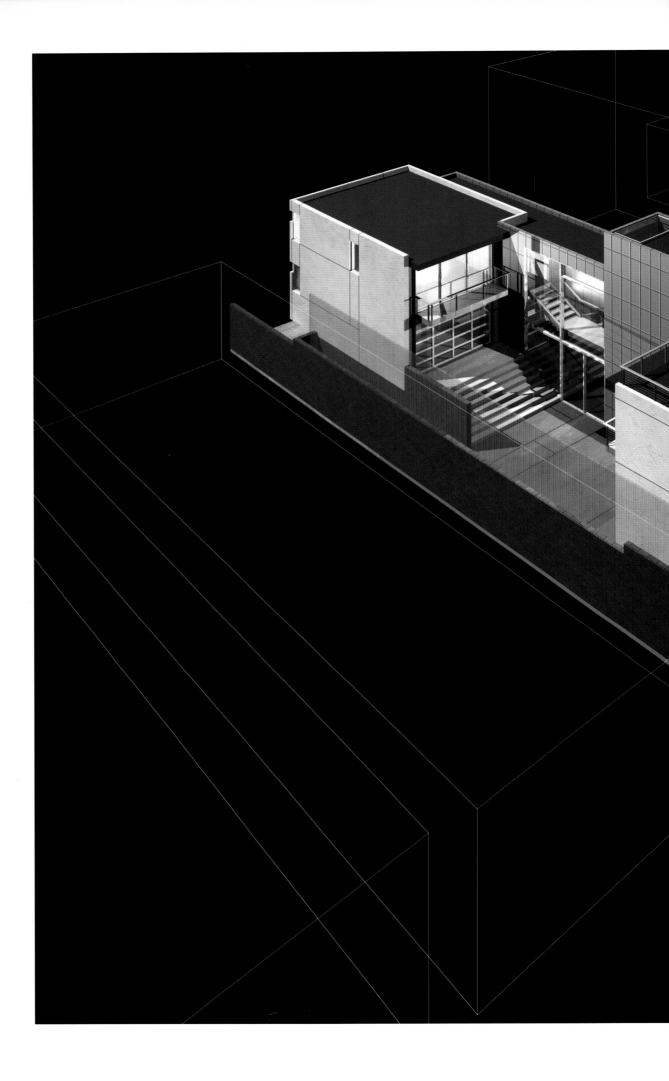

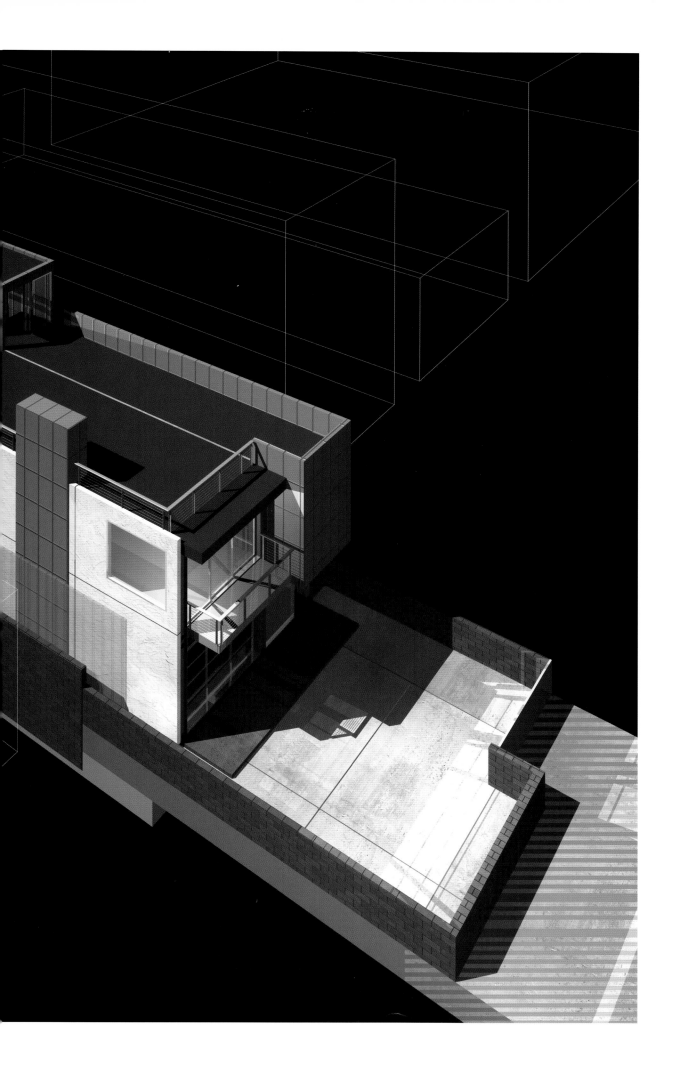

ROYER HOUSE

Another new Venice house, this property is clearly visible from two sides and is designed for lively interaction with the tight-knit community that has grown up around a grid of six canals—all that survive from the initial layout of this community, nearly a century ago. Skinny lots extend from service roads in back to public footpaths along the waterways, and the challenge is to pull in light from narrow setbacks to either side to balance the openness of the façade without sacrificing privacy. The Royers were able to acquire the last vacant lot at a junction of two canals, and Ehrlich and Schmidt have taken full

advantage of this. They mark the corner with a two-story glass pavilion that opens up through sliders to the front yard. As on Ehrlich's own exposed corner site, setbacks provide terraces, the roof is tilted to add height, and the stucco façade is complemented with a cladding of white corrugated steel. Its undulations pick up on the rippling surface of the canals, and serve, along with the reflective expanses of glass and the projecting pergolas, to diminish the bulk of this 3000-square-foot house.

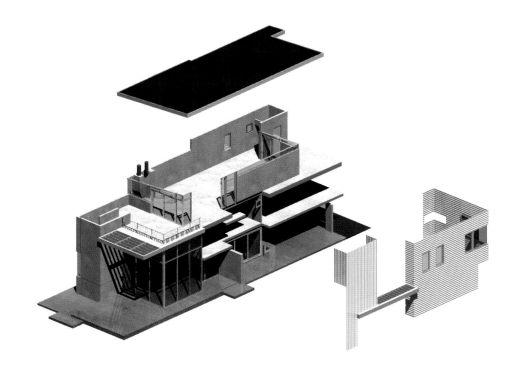

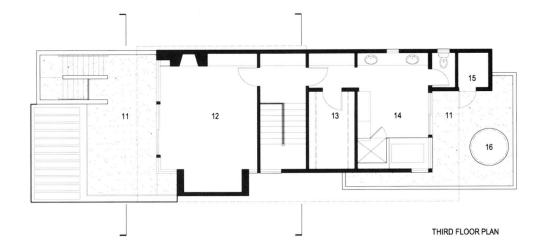

THIRD FLOOR PLAN

1. LIVING ROOM
2. ENTRY
3. DINING ROOM
4. POWDER ROOM
5. KITCHEN
6. GARAGE
7. LIBRARY
8. LAUNDRY
9. BATHROOM
10. BEDROOM
11. DECK
12. MASTER BEDROOM
13. CLOSET
14. MASTER BATHROOM
15. STORAGE
16. SPA
17. OPEN TO BELOW

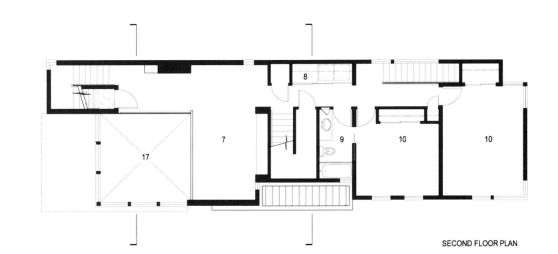

SECOND FLOOR PLAN

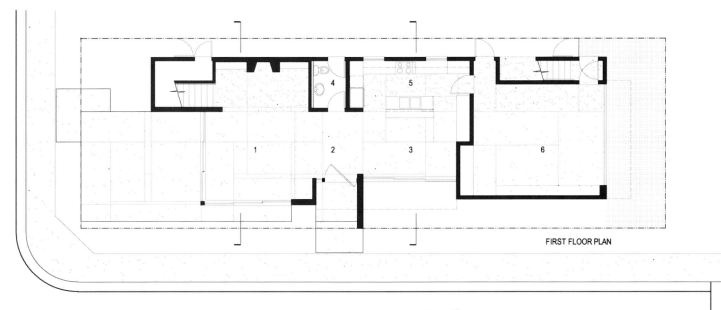

FIRST FLOOR PLAN

N

0   2'   4'   8'   16'

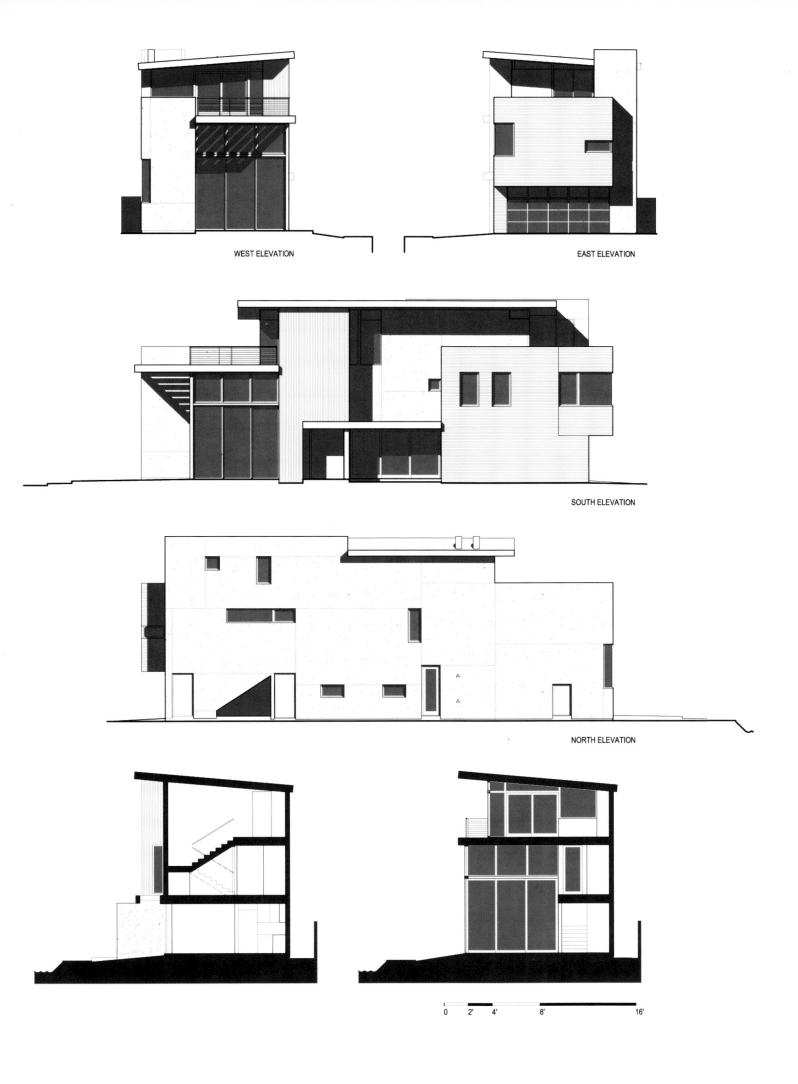

WEST ELEVATION

EAST ELEVATION

SOUTH ELEVATION

NORTH ELEVATION

0   2'   4'   8'   16'

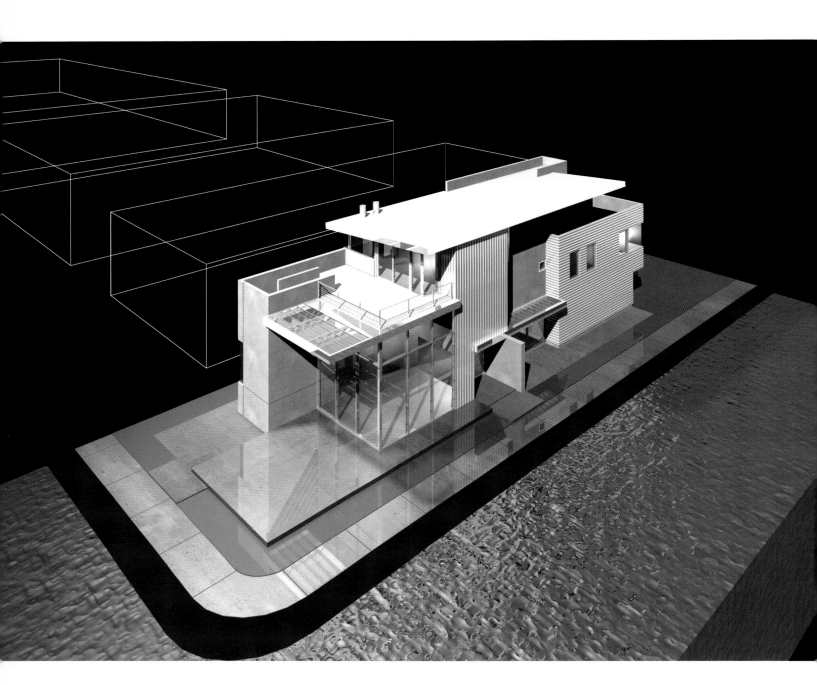

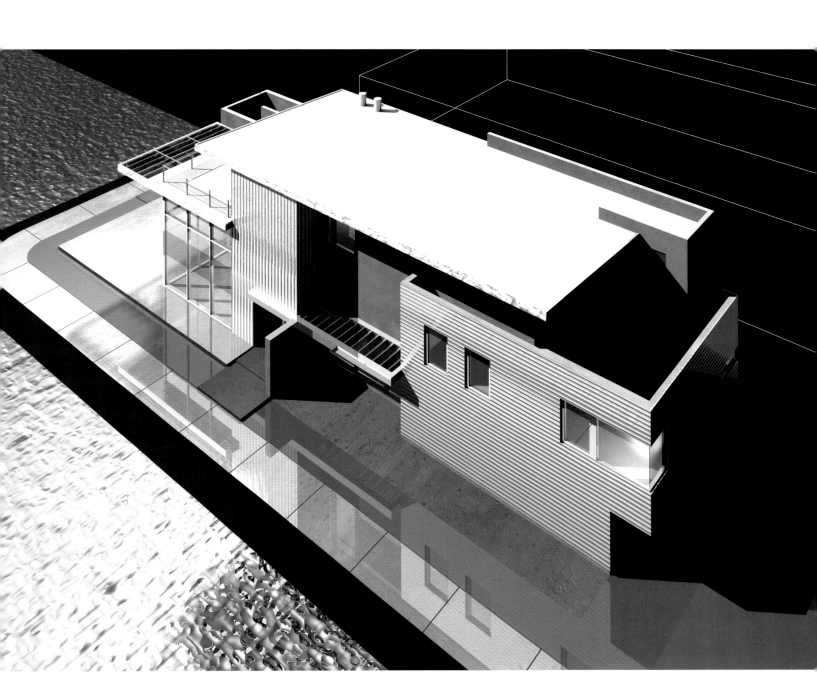

BEACH LOFTS

As the Royer house took shape, Ehrlich completed work on a mid-block row of four town houses a few steps from Venice beach. The site is sandwiched between two apartment buildings and the challenge was to provide maximum living space within the permitted envelope without engendering a sense of claustrophobia. The solution was to set the row four feet above ground on a concrete deck that serves as an entry terrace with parking below. Applying the lessons of their single-family homes, the architects used a bamboo fence to enclose both sides of the terrace and screen out the neighbors, and clad the wood-frame structure with gray–green dashcoat stucco and corrugated steel painted a pale gray.

The concept of an industrial loft, inspired by the gritty context, is carried inside. A single high volume is lit from big windows on both sides and a pop-up roof lantern. Mezzanine galleries at front and back are linked by a catwalk of steel grating, and sandblasted steel panels alternate with drywall and exposed wood and steel beams. The floors are of polished concrete. Roll-up glass doors open onto front decks and a roof terrace provides an unbroken ocean view over the neighboring block. The limitations of the confined site have been overcome, and the mix of raw finishes and refined details impart an individuality to these repetitive units.

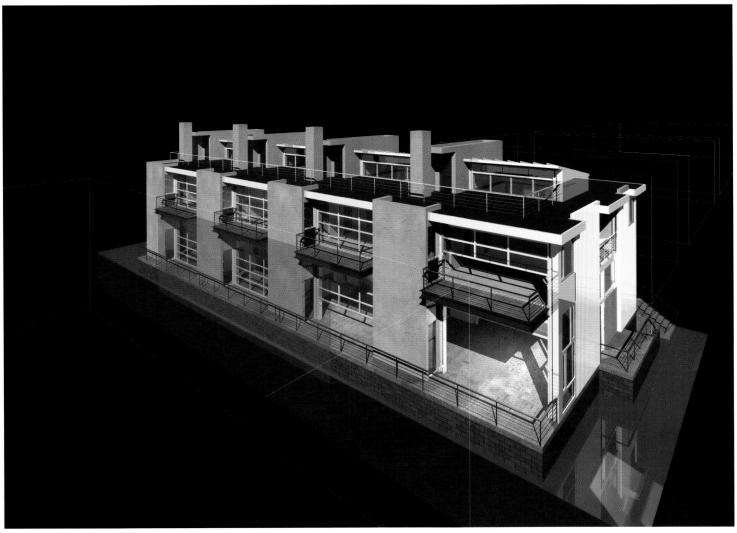

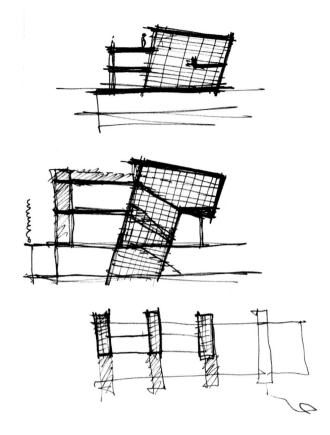

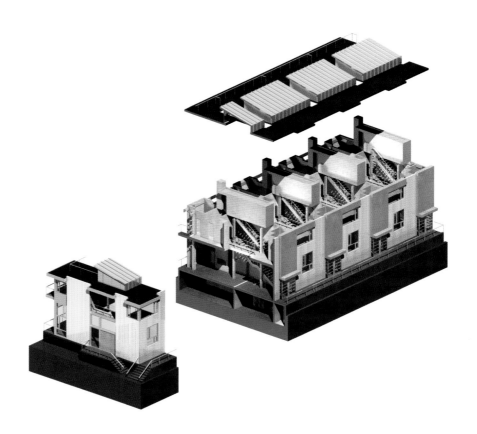

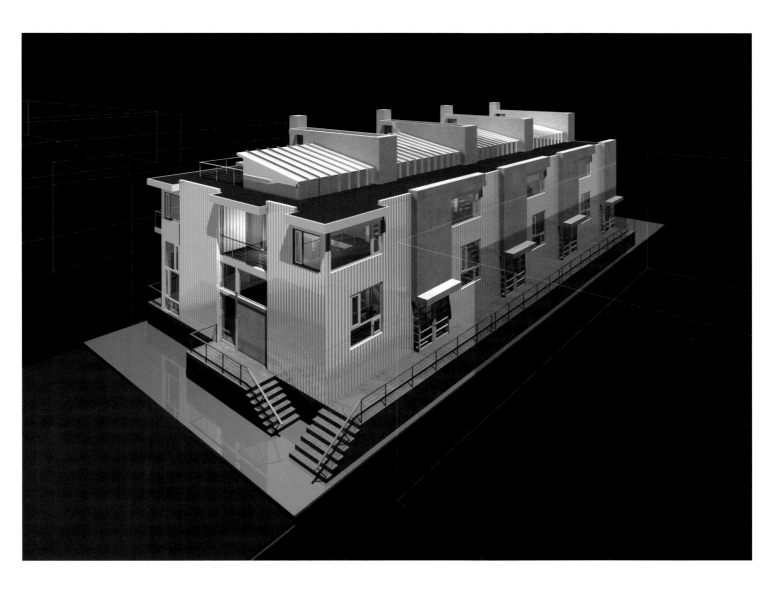

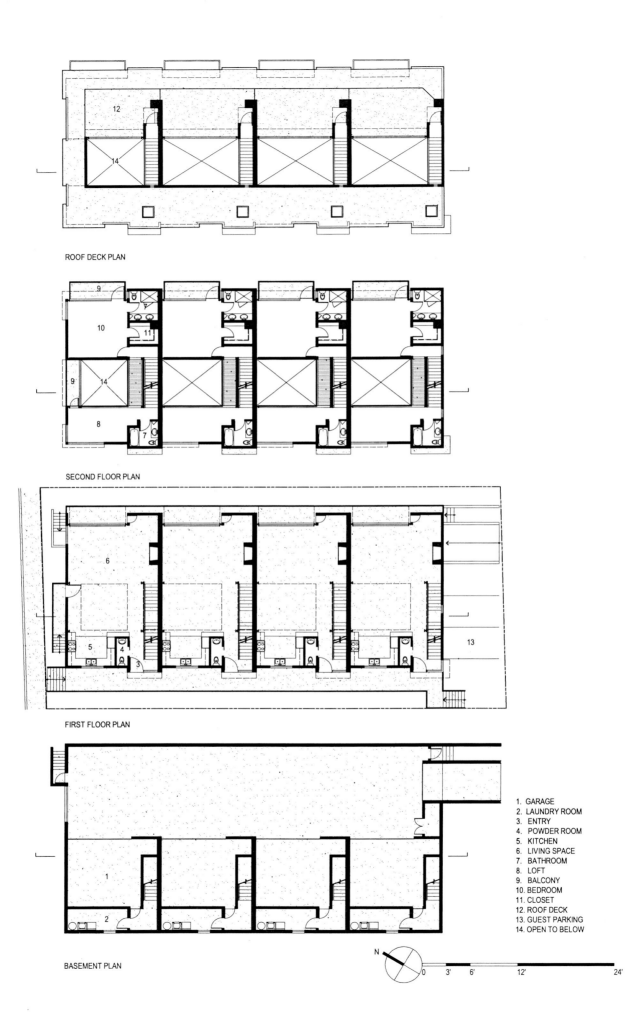

ROOF DECK PLAN

SECOND FLOOR PLAN

FIRST FLOOR PLAN

BASEMENT PLAN

1. GARAGE
2. LAUNDRY ROOM
3. ENTRY
4. POWDER ROOM
5. KITCHEN
6. LIVING SPACE
7. BATHROOM
8. LOFT
9. BALCONY
10. BEDROOM
11. CLOSET
12. ROOF DECK
13. GUEST PARKING
14. OPEN TO BELOW

N

0   3'   6'   12'   24'

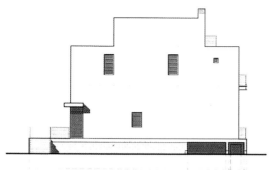

NORTH ELEVATION

SOUTH ELEVATION

WEST ELEVATION

EAST ELEVATION

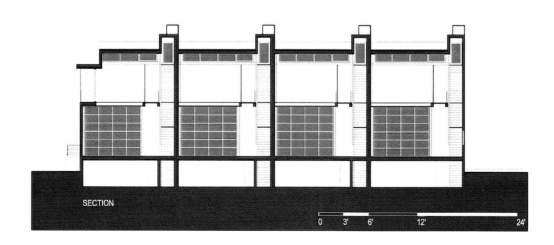

SECTION

0   3'   6'   12'   24'

NEUTRA ADDITION

Sandwiched between palm-fringed palisades and gleaming sand is the classic modern beach house that Richard Neutra built for Albert Lewin, the producer of 'Mutiny on the Bounty' and 'The Good Earth', a literate writer-director, and an enthusiastic collector of modern art. Sixty years after its completion in 1938, Ehrlich restored and extended it onto the neighboring lot for a couple who collect vintage modern furniture. He had launched his practice in 1981 with the Kalfus studio, a white modernist cube in the garden of Neutra's Loring house in the Hollywood Hills; here the challenge was to create a much larger addition that would flow out of the taut glass and stucco original, while respecting its materials and proportions.

Ehrlich and Schmidt extruded a guest suite over a rebuilt garage, achieving a seamless join with the original structure, and extended the housekeeper's apartment over a second double garage with brushed stainless doors, creating an impassive new facade of white stucco and poured concrete that helps shut out the roar of traffic from the busy coast highway. Behind this addition, floating like an ark in a sea of grass, is a pavilion with a stainless-steel cycloidal vault, perforated on the underside to absorb sound, which was inspired by the roofs of Louis Kahn's Kimbell Art Museum in Fort Worth. It subtly echoes the rounded glass bay of the house, to which it is linked by a glass walkway. To dematerialize this massive structure, it is supported on slender steel outrigger columns on the side nearest the house, and the glass walls at either end can be fully retracted to open the interior to ocean breezes. The inner side is also of glass; to the south, poured concrete walls define the boundary of the site and enclose a kitchen/buffet and a bathroom. The concrete floor was acid-washed to achieve varied textures.

The architects used the new structure to enhance the old and to siphon off the boisterous activities of the beach and the owners' small son. A strong axis flows from a grassy court through the pavilion and a new pool to a motorized gate in the garden wall. This glides open to reveal the beach and frame a lifeguard station, turning a private courtyard into an extension of the public beach. The brushed stainless and concrete have greater density than the silver-trimmed stucco, but employ the same restrained palette. "I've drawn on 60 years of technology to make Neutra's dream come true and to achieve a balance of the serene and the kinetic," says Ehrlich.

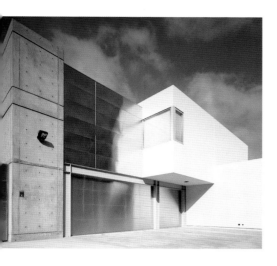

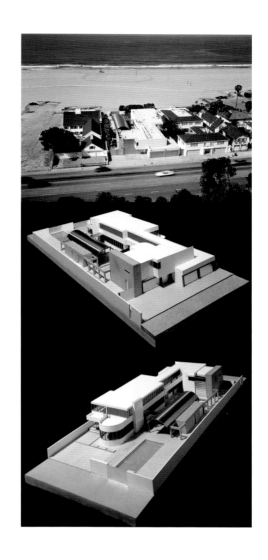

12/55

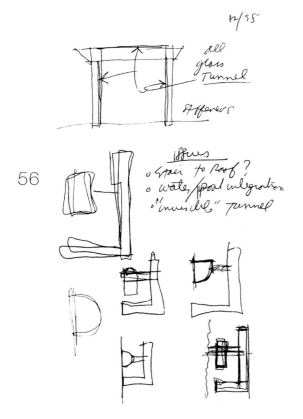

all
glass
Tunnel

stiffeners

issues
o stair to Roof?
o water/pool integration
o "invisible" Tunnel

56

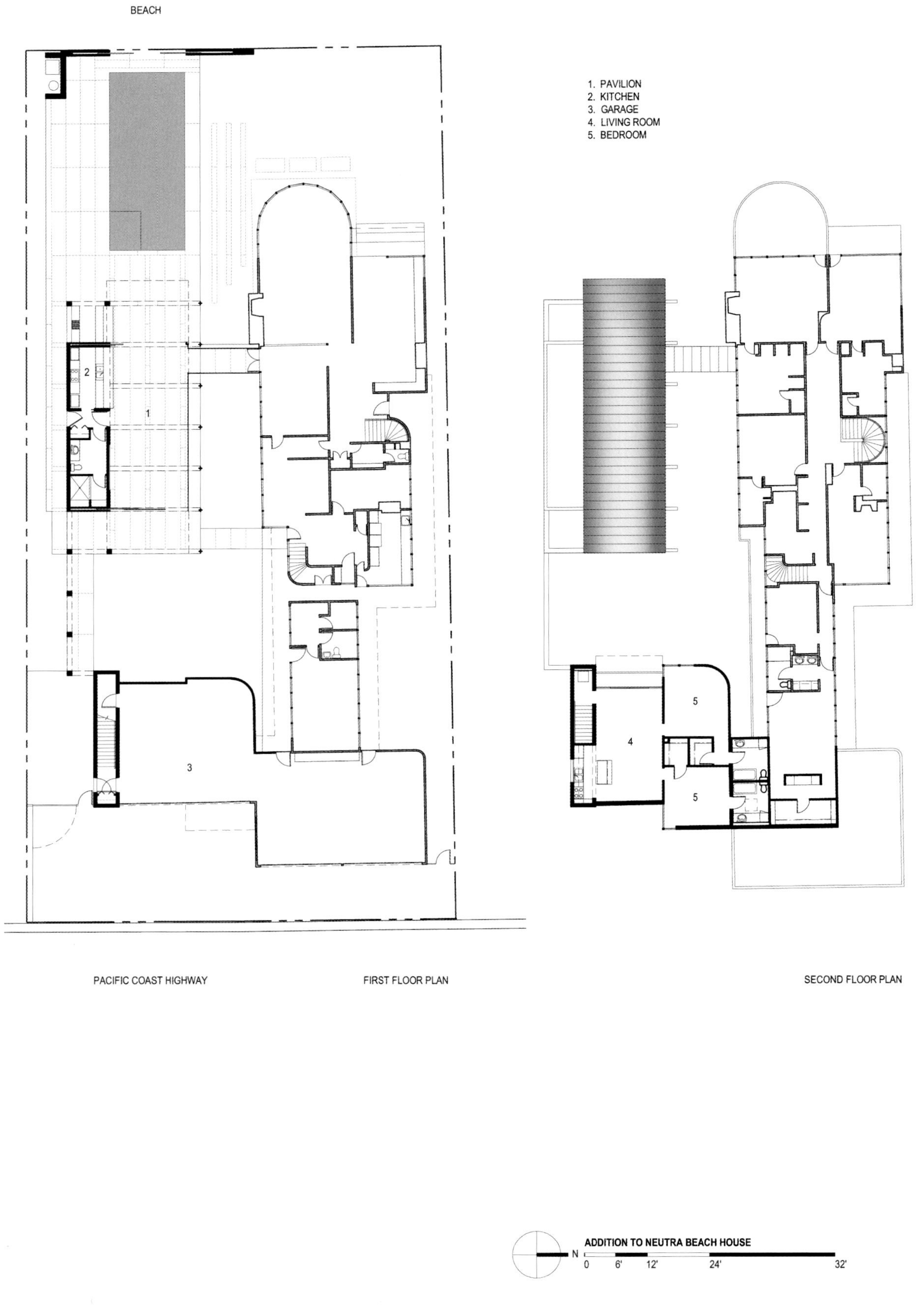

BEACH

1. PAVILION
2. KITCHEN
3. GARAGE
4. LIVING ROOM
5. BEDROOM

58

2

1

3

PACIFIC COAST HIGHWAY

FIRST FLOOR PLAN

5

4

5

SECOND FLOOR PLAN

N

ADDITION TO NEUTRA BEACH HOUSE

0   6'   12'   24'   32'

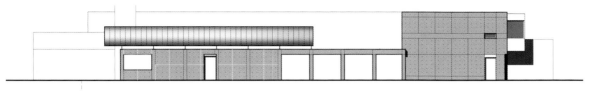

EAST ELEVATION

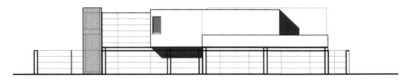

NORTH ELEVATION

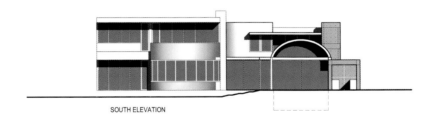

SOUTH ELEVATION

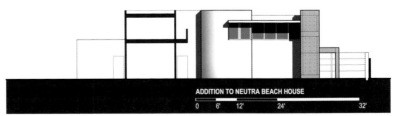

ADDITION TO NEUTRA BEACH HOUSE

0   6'   12'   24'   32'

SOUTH COURTYARD ELEVATION

pool

16

PATIO

Setb

Bath

kitchen
to
Fireplace?

62

internal
st...

Ext
Storge

concrete
wall & ...

Water
Scrub

0

16

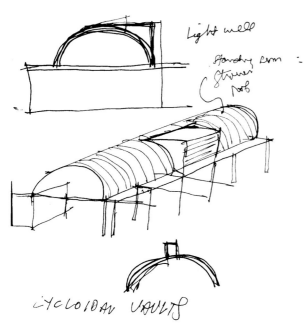

light well

standing room
standing
$\dots$

CYCLOIDAL VAULTS

WOODS HOUSE

Transforming the Lewin residence was as demanding an assignment as the design of a major new house; upgrading the Woods house in Santa Monica Canyon required bold moves on a modest scale, for the 1950s structure that rises three stories from a precipitous slope was cramped and inconvenient. In 1985, Eddie and Jan Woods hired the local firm of Mulder Katkov to add a deck and replace the wood facing with steel-troweled concrete; however they went no further and kept the house chiefly for its spectacular view. To enlarge and reconfigure the interior, they turned to Ehrlich, who had taught architecture to Jan at UCLA. He added 750 square feet at one end of the house (an increase of 25 per cent), to provide a new living room on the main level and a new master bathroom above. The street façade was refaced with gray-green steel-troweled stucco and horizontally scored aluminum to weave the old fabric and the addition together. The interior was gutted; walls came down, ceilings were raised, windows and doors were repositioned. The kitchen—now

a sophisticated composition of maple cabinets and granite counter tops—was relocated so that it opens onto the broadest section of the deck and is easily accessible for alfresco dining.

Encouraged by the owners' minimal taste, the architects installed polished concrete and pale oak floors, a curved soffit that links the dining area to the new sitting area a few steps down, and a ledge of granite extending from the fireplace the full width of the room. In the master suite, broad floor boards carry one into the new bathroom through double doors of laminated glass, and this axis is reinforced by a ledge of limestone that moves from hearth to shower by way of the tub in an unbroken sweep. The cool palette and the classic steel, glass and pale leather furniture subtly enhance an interior that seems to have been carved from solid blocks of stone and stucco. Every form emerges from another and echoes the rest, achieving a serene flow of space on both levels.

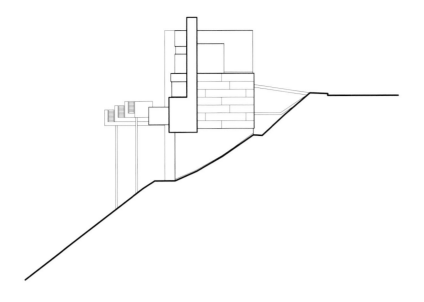

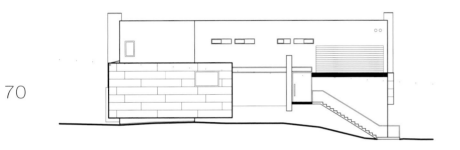

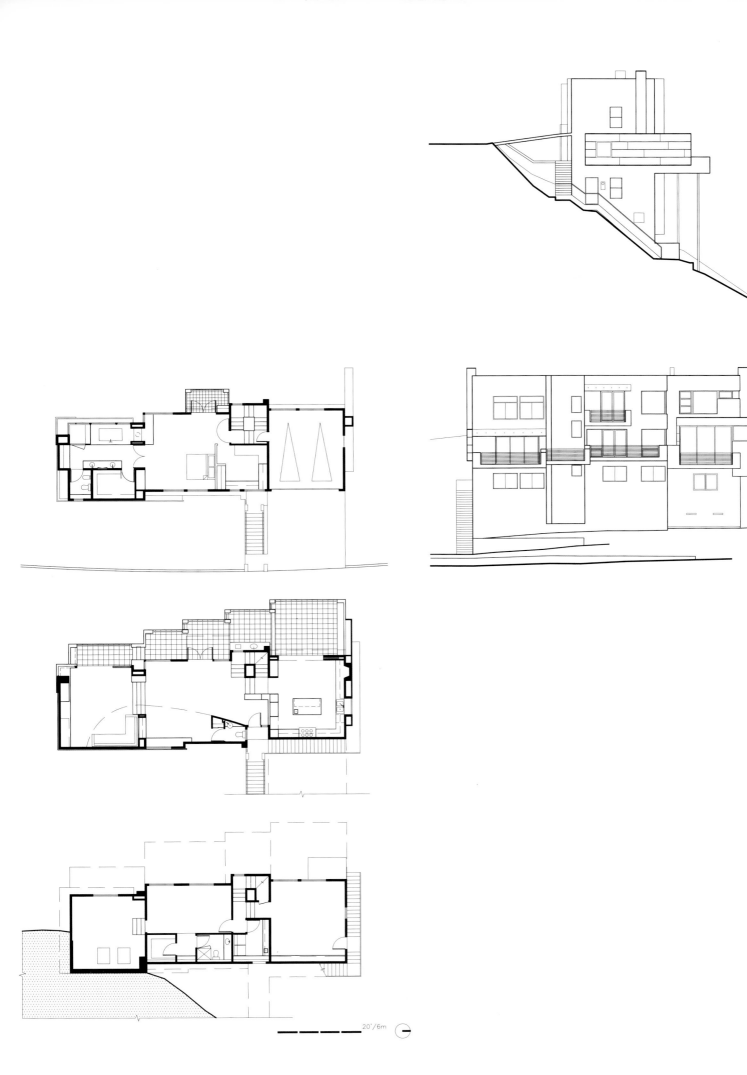

20'/6m

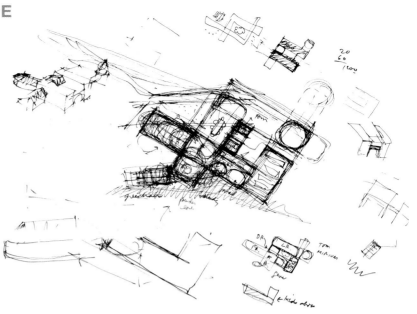

SCHULMAN HOUSE

74

Ehrlich made his reputation, as most architects do, with modest buildings on difficult lots. When the Schulmans asked him to design a large house with a generous budget he was ready, and their enthusiasm for the clean lines and free-flowing spaces of modern classics by Neutra and Schindler made for a productive relationship. After interviewing other architects who offered them a menu of styles, this young couple admired the integrity of one who showed them his work and said: "This is the kind of house I build. If you like it, I'm your man; if not, you shouldn't hire me."

The essentials of the plan evolved from a lively owner-architect dialogue: two-story wings containing family rooms below and bedrooms above are linked by a double-height living/entertaining room and upper-level bridge. These wings reach forward in a welcoming embrace to frame a landscaped entrance court. "I was used to designing houses on tight, hillside lots," says the architect. "I drew on that experience to locate the house in the neck of the canyon and bury the garage in the hillside, in order to preserve as much as possible of the

meadow behind." The siting was also dictated by the need to preserve an old sycamore in front, and a big coral tree to the rear.

"In architecture, you try to find a sense of order in what the client and the site tell you," says Ehrlich. "And when you've discovered it you can expand on it." As the design evolved over the next eight months, he discovered creative ways to energize what began as a symmetrical H plan. The east wing was splayed 17 degrees outwards to align it with that side of the canyon, imparting dynamic energy to the forecourt and to the interior. The architect brought to this level site the spatial drama and asymmetrical interlocking volumes of the hillside Gold–Friedman house, combining these with a calm monumentality that integrates it with the landscape. The insistent horizontality of the glazing bars, steel balustrades, and grooved concrete complements the verticality of the principal volumes to create a harmonious balance of opposing forces.

There is a richer sense of materiality than Ehrlich had been able to achieve before. Concrete, poured into forms that were lined

with plastic laminate to achieve a satiny finish, complements white stucco planes on the façade and is employed to stunning effect in the stair hall. (Ehrlich overcame the clients' concern that it would look like a freeway by promising to cover it with stucco at his own expense if they didn't like it after a year.) Red mahogany and copper trim on the roof planes add warmth to the crisp geometry.

Staircases—one enclosed, one open—lead up to the bedrooms and the bridge that cuts across the central void. Taut ribbons of silvery steel form the balustrades and play off the mahogany floors and sleek maple cabinets. One's gaze is drawn up and out through the great window of this lofty central space. Sliding doors open to the forecourt or the landscaped garden, and every part of the house amplifies this dialogue of indoors and out, from the sweeping vistas experienced on the bridge to the wash of sunlight from skylights and clerestories across white stucco walls.

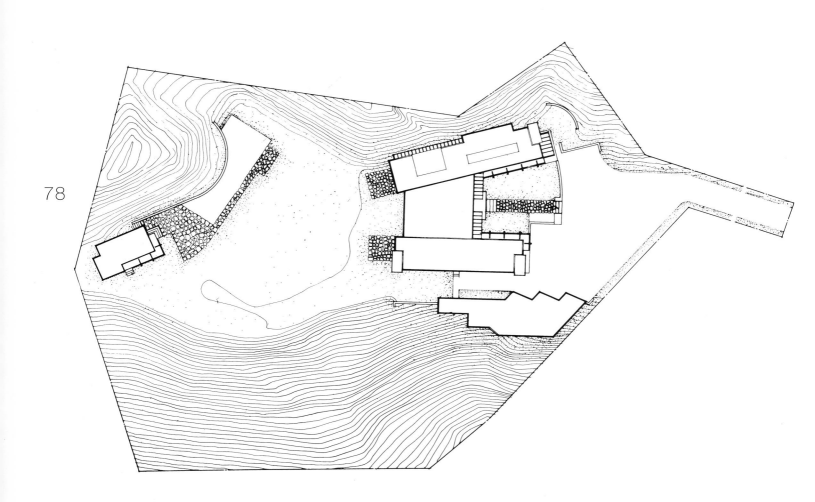

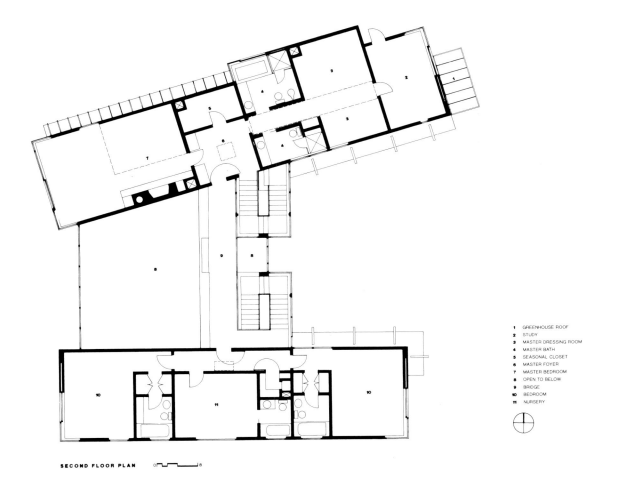

SECOND FLOOR PLAN   0 ⌐_⌐_⌐ 8

1 GREENHOUSE ROOF
2 STUDY
3 MASTER DRESSING ROOM
4 MASTER BATH
5 SEASONAL CLOSET
6 MASTER FOYER
7 MASTER BEDROOM
8 OPEN TO BELOW
9 BRIDGE
10 BEDROOM
11 NURSERY

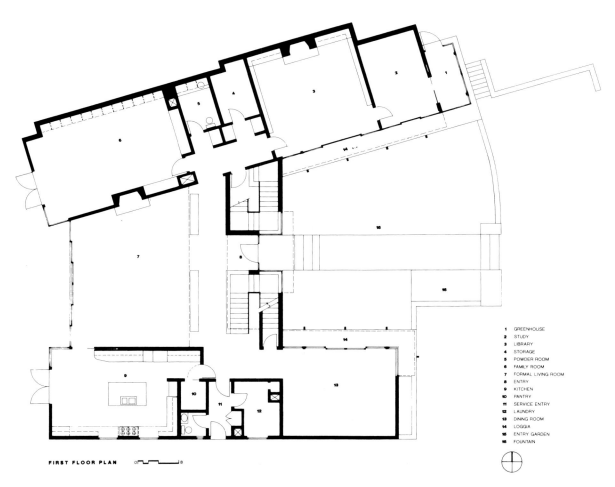

FIRST FLOOR PLAN   0 ⌐_⌐_⌐ 8

1 GREENHOUSE
2 STUDY
3 LIBRARY
4 STORAGE
5 POWDER ROOM
6 FAMILY ROOM
7 FORMAL LIVING ROOM
8 ENTRY
9 KITCHEN
10 PANTRY
11 SERVICE ENTRY
12 LAUNDRY
13 DINING ROOM
14 LOGGIA
15 ENTRY GARDEN
16 FOUNTAIN

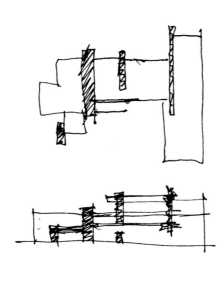

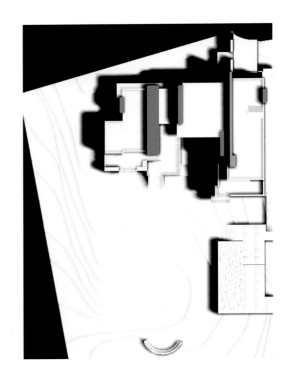

CANYON HOUSE

The next major residential commission after the Schulman house also occupies a leafy canyon on the Westside of LA, and replaced an existing house. However, the Canyon house is set on a hillside and employs a similar footprint to the old in order to preserve towering sycamores at front and back. Massive walls containing service spaces rhythmically punctuate an asymmetrical, three-level complex of cubes that dances down the slope with flights of steps extending like amphitheaters into the landscape. So fluid and free-spirited is the house, one would never suspect that its boundary lines were predetermined by the need to save trees.

The vertical masses slice through the house front to back and are clad in stucco that is slashed and integrally colored in tones that were inspired by the amazing palette of wet sycamore bark—from olive greens and grays,

to yellow ocher, burnt siena and brown-purple. Each wall has a distinct hue, which roots it in the ground and brings the landscape into the house, and the rich textures were influenced by Jackson Pollock paintings that Ehrlich saw in an exhibition at this time. The projecting copper-clad roof planes and ironwood decks slide in and out like drawers in a chest, complementing the vertical elements. The third dimension is supplied by the planes of white stucco that shield the house from the street and the full height glazing of the principal rooms to the rear.

One enters the house at midlevel and the great room serves as a crossroads. Niches for sculpture and a tilted oculus framing treetops punctuate one wall; stair treads project from another, leading up to the master suite. The walls are cut away and space floats around

them, contained by the horizontal glazing bars, and liberated by the mitered glass corners and pocketing sliders framed in Douglas fir. Rooted yet open, the interior is a perfect match for the dynamic structure. This is the house that Schindler never got to build and though it has the complex spatial geometry of de Stijl, it is far bolder in its expression than anything Rietveld or van Doesberg essayed.

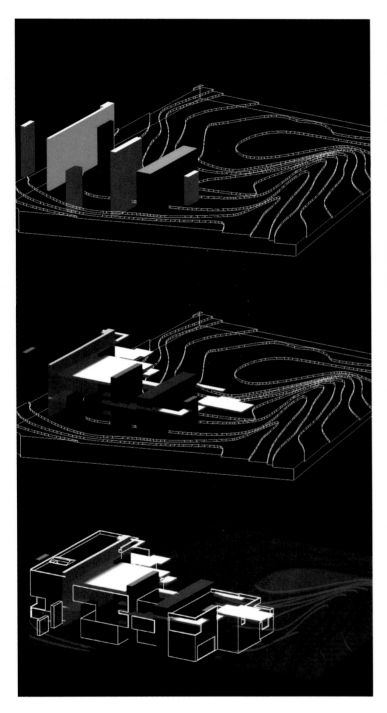
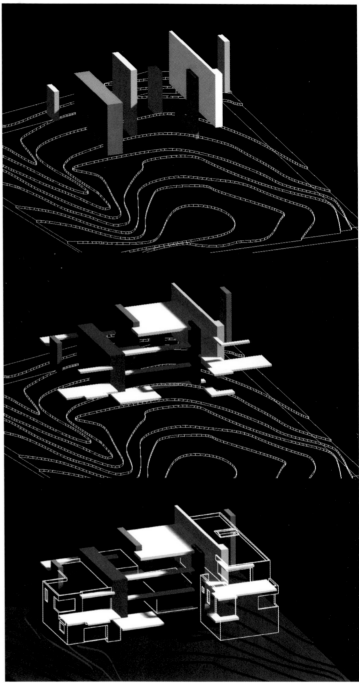

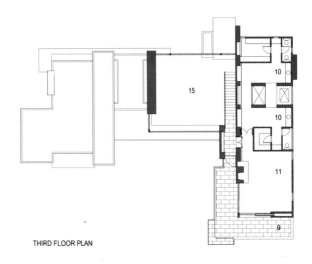

THIRD FLOOR PLAN

SECOND FLOOR PLAN

1. ENTRY
2. LIVING ROOM
3. LIBRARY
4. DINING ROOM
5. KITCHEN
6. MEDIA ROOM
7. OFFICE
8. GARAGE
9. DECK
10. MASTER BATHROOM
11. MASTER BEDROOM
12. BEDROOM
13. STORAGE
14. MECHANICAL ROOM
15. OPEN TO BELOW
16. EXERCISE ROOM
17. LAUNDRY

FIRST FLOOR PLAN

N

CANYON RESIDENCE

0   6'   12'   24'   32'

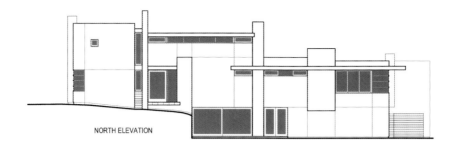

NORTH ELEVATION

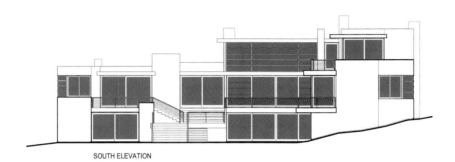

SOUTH ELEVATION

WEST ELEVATION

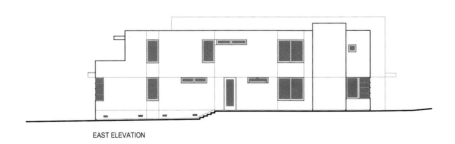

EAST ELEVATION

CANYON RESIDENCE

0   6'   12'   24'   32'

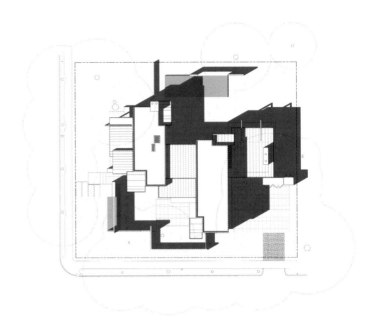

WALDFOGEL HOUSE

An expansive house in Palo Alto occupies a flat, half-acre site and takes its cues from the urbanity of the community and the sophistication of the couple who commissioned it. In contrast to the Schulman and Canyon houses, which span their plots from side to side, have impassive entry façades and face out to lush gardens, Ehrlich and Schmidt designed this house to open on all sides with a pinwheel plan that embraces peripheral courtyards. The massing is more complex, the horizontal and vertical planes are tauter and more pared down. Extended roof planes are clad in charcoal gray Rhinezinc, an alloy imported from Germany, which is carried into the house. As in the houses Mies designed in Europe in the 1920s, one half expects the precisely tooled geometry to click into motion and the slender planes to glide away like the entry gate.

The approach leads past a wall of water, and the entrance court doubles as a terrace for the lofty dining room that links the two halves of the house. The living room and the husband's study to the north share another paved court extending out to the garden, and the kitchen and family room to the south open onto a pool. An axial wall of poured concrete that bisects the house evokes a primal hearth and is carved out and cut away like those in the Canyon residence. At the upper level, a frosted glass bridge links the master suite and the wife's study to the child's and guest bedrooms. Alternately grand and intimate, the interior spaces seem to wrap around you and to frame varied perspectives.

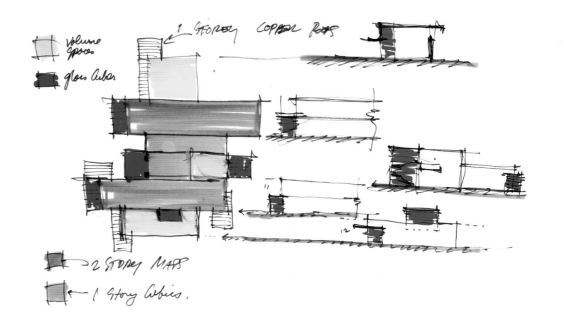

volume spaces

glass cubes

2 STOREY COPPER ROOFS

2 STOREY MASS

1 Story cubics.

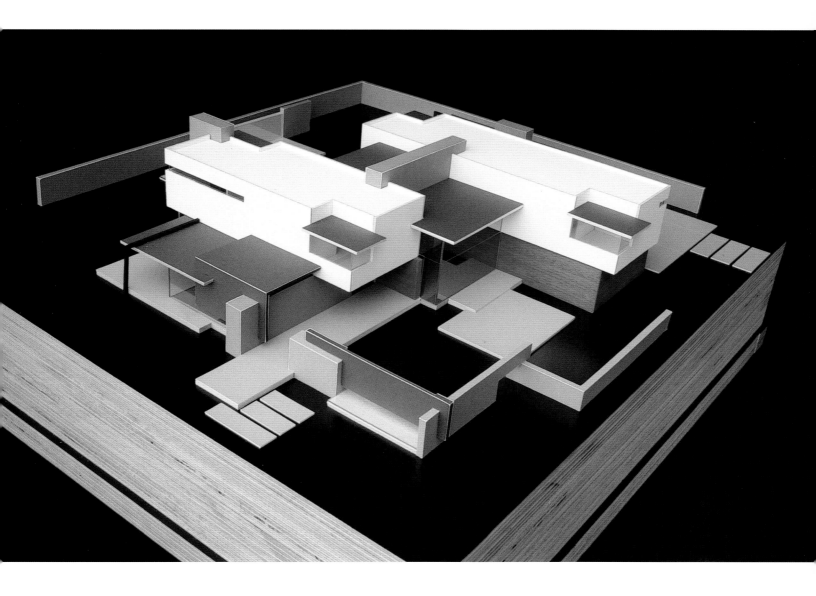

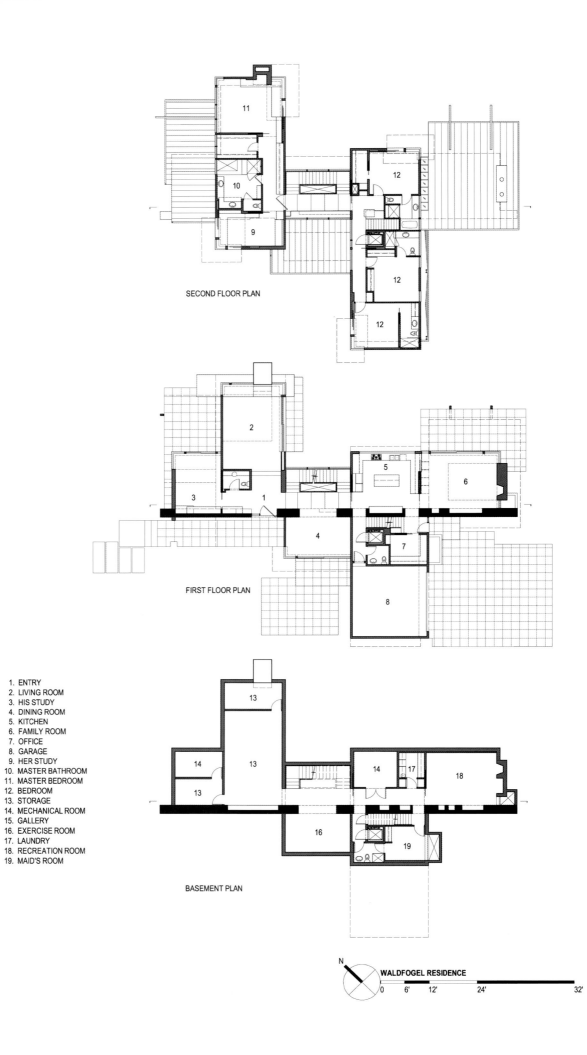

SECOND FLOOR PLAN

FIRST FLOOR PLAN

1. ENTRY
2. LIVING ROOM
3. HIS STUDY
4. DINING ROOM
5. KITCHEN
6. FAMILY ROOM
7. OFFICE
8. GARAGE
9. HER STUDY
10. MASTER BATHROOM
11. MASTER BEDROOM
12. BEDROOM
13. STORAGE
14. MECHANICAL ROOM
15. GALLERY
16. EXERCISE ROOM
17. LAUNDRY
18. RECREATION ROOM
19. MAID'S ROOM

BASEMENT PLAN

N

WALDFOGEL RESIDENCE

0   6'   12'   24'   32'

NORTH ELEVATION

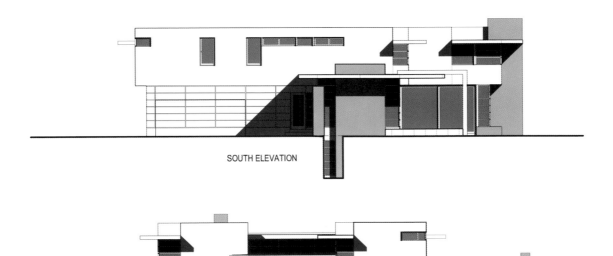

SOUTH ELEVATION

WEST ELEVATION

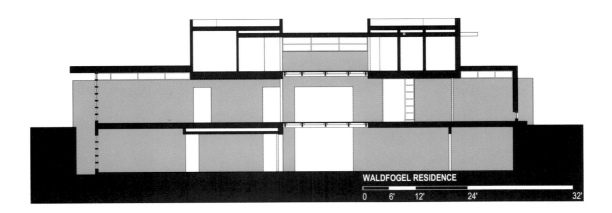

EAST ELEVATION

WALDFOGEL RESIDENCE

0   6'   12'   24'   32'

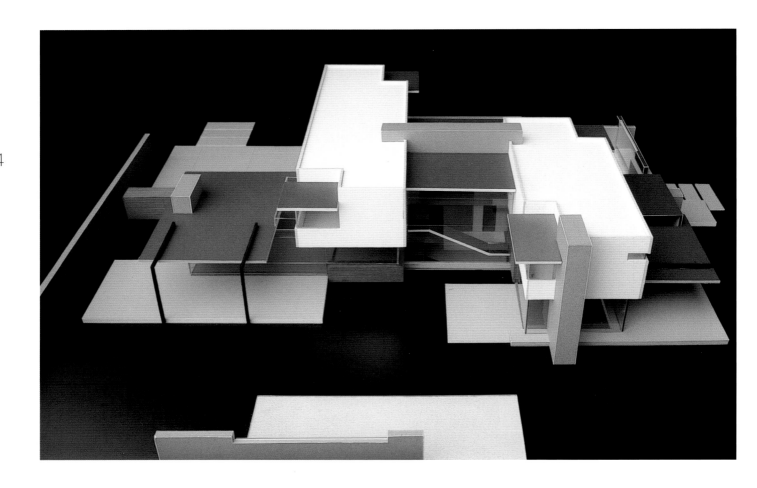

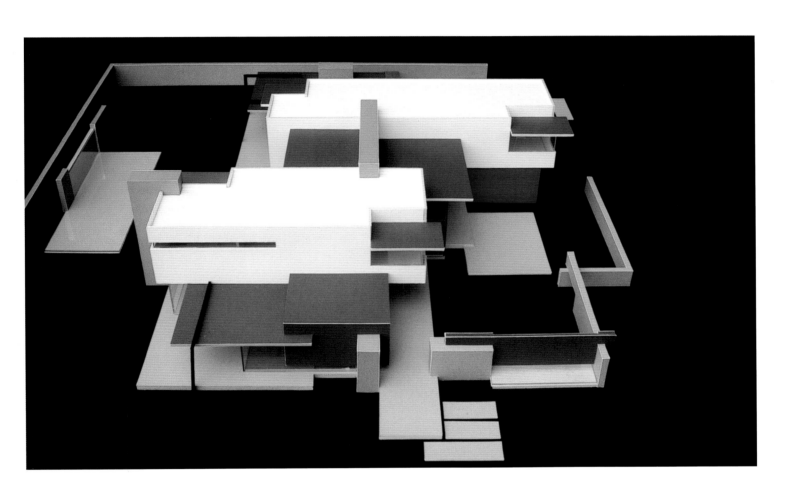

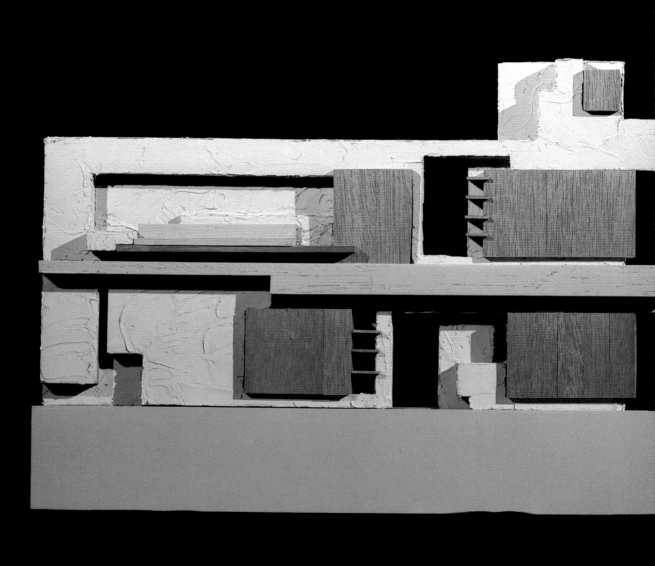

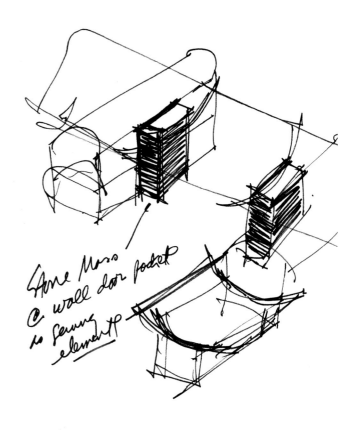

DUBAI HOUSE

By far the most ambitious of recent projects is the family compound that Ehrlich and Schmidt are designing for the head of a leading family in Dubai, for a site in that oil-rich city state on the Persian Gulf. At 35,000 square feet it is almost as large as all the other houses in this book put together, and the desert location and ferocious heat could not be more different from the temperate landscapes of southern California. And yet, the lucidity of its plan and the sensitivity of its response to the needs of client and culture, are entirely compatible with the firm's earlier work, which is why they were chosen.

The client asked the LA office of Gensler, the firm that designs branches of his bank, to recommend a Californian architect who could create a hybrid of Western and Islamic ideas. After long consideration, the client made his choice and invited the architects to develop their concept during a week-long charette. "I don't want this to be like a house in Malibu or Florida—it has to be rooted in my culture," he told them. "That resonated with me, having lived and worked in Africa," says Ehrlich. "But this was a highly sophisticated

project, and the budget allowed me to experiment with new techniques and materials." He and Schmidt searched for a way of protecting the living quarters from the relentless sun that would also serve as an apt metaphor for the whole.

His inspiration was to loft a huge arced canopy, sheathed in titanium and supported on a double row of stone-clad steel columns, over rows of simple two-story buildings with flat rooftop sleeping decks in the desert vernacular tradition. The canopy is as expansive as a football field but its section is that of a crescent moon, the symbol of new life that tops the minarets of Islam. It also suggests an inverted tent—a reference to Bedouin forbears—and is pierced along the north edge to cast barred shadows. The pool of shade lowers the temperature and channels the breezes, and the columns double as mechanical exhaust vents that project up through the canopy.

Cross axes of water and palm trees, evoking desert oases, separate the buildings which extend beyond the canopy and are further

protected by a curved moucharabie, the traditional pierced sunscreen that is reinterpreted here in stainless steel. The three-part plan separates the reception area (majlis) for male guests at the east end, from the women's behind the central grand hall and the family's sleeping quarters to the west. Luxuriant plantings, fountains and reflecting pools, shady courtyards and terraces will surround and penetrate these buildings—a paradise garden set in a desert.

From Africa to Japan, and California to the Arabian Peninsula, Ehrlich has journeyed far. And yet, whatever and wherever he is invited to build, his vision remains constant, his principles uncompromised. Houses are an essential part of a practice that continues to grow but never loses touch with its roots. In shaping a house that is ideal for a single family, he develops ideas that enrich his public buildings and may lead on to multiple housing. The end of the journey is not in sight.

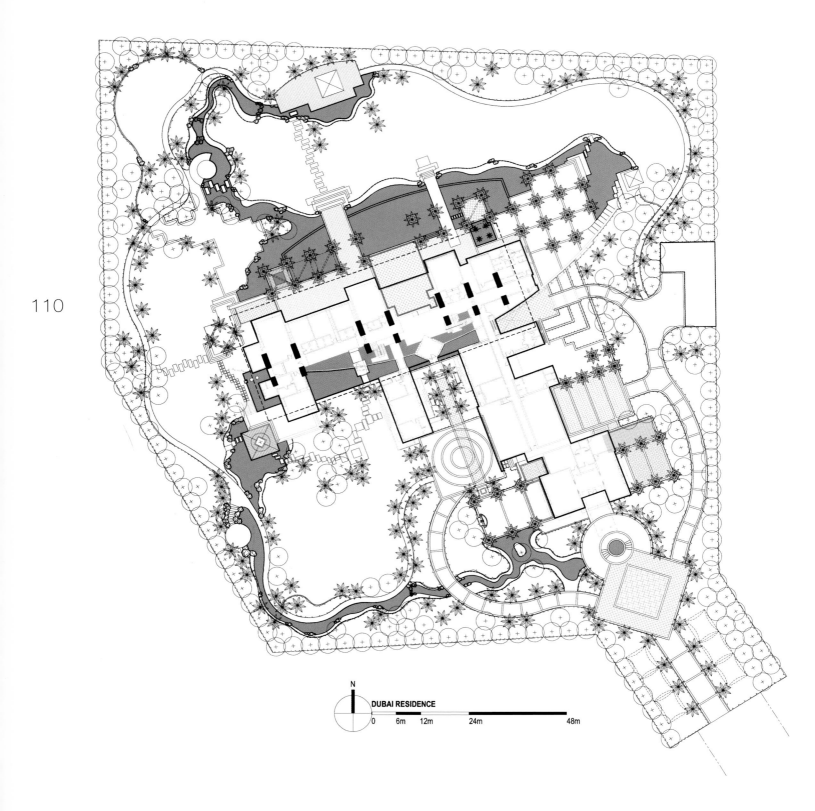

N

DUBAI RESIDENCE

0   6m   12m   24m   48m

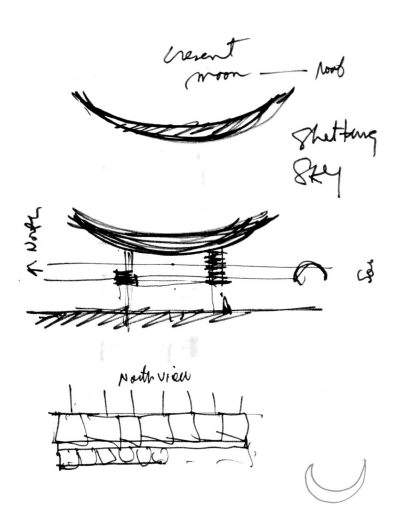

cresent
moon ——— roof

shelling
sky

↑ north

co

North view

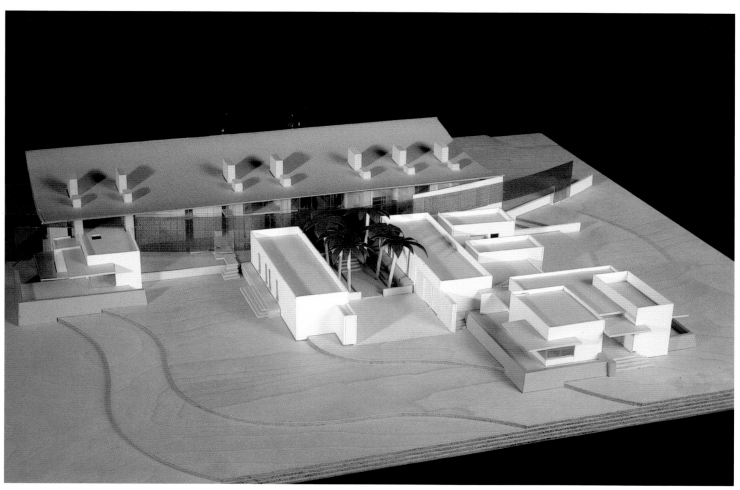

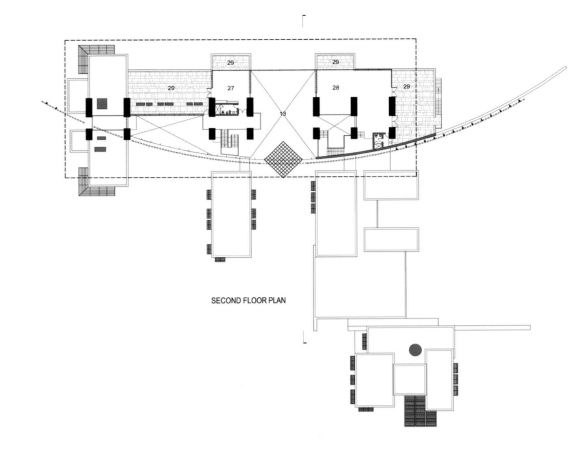

SECOND FLOOR PLAN

1   ENTRY
2   GRAND HALL
3   WOMEN'S MAJILIS
4   DINING ROOM
5   KITCHEN
6   FAMILY ROOM
7   PLAY ROOM
8   GARDEN HALL
9   MASTER BEDROOM
10 DRESSING ROOM
11 BEDROOM
12 REFLECTING POOL
13 OPEN TO BELOW
14 MEN'S CHANGING
15 WOMEN'S CHANGING
16 LAUNDRY ROOM
17 MAJILIS ENTRY
18 MAJILIS
19 DINING ROOM
20 OFFICE
21 BUTLER'S PANTRY
22 GUEST LIVING ROOM
23 GUEST BEDROOM
24 OUTDOOR KITCHEN
25 MEN'S WAITING
26 GARAGE
27 BONUS ROOM
28 EXERCISE ROOM
29 ROOF DECK

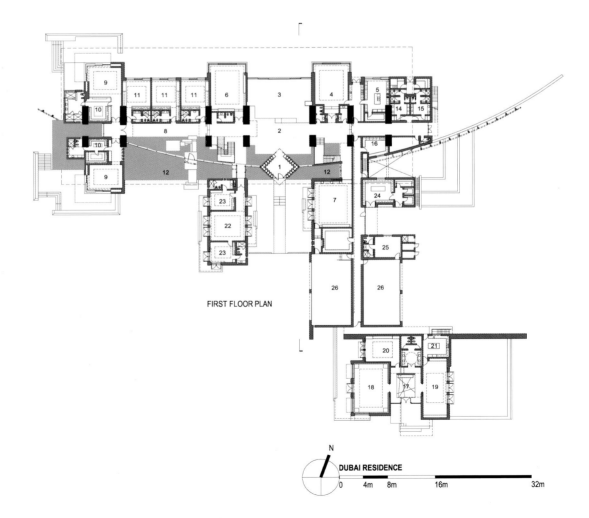

FIRST FLOOR PLAN

N

DUBAI RESIDENCE

0   4m 8m   16m   32m

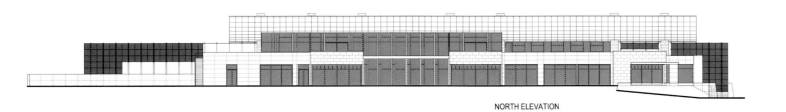

NORTH ELEVATION

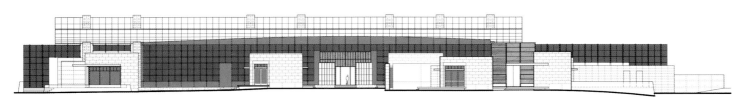

SOUTH ELEVATION

EAST ELEVATION

WEST ELEVATION

DUBAI RESIDENCE

0   4m   8m   16m   32m

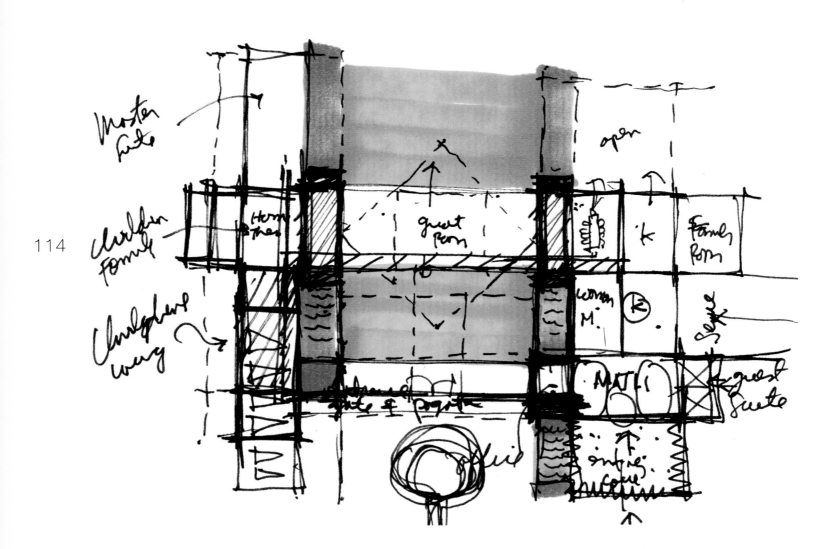

Master suite

Children Family

Christopher wing

Home theater

great room

open

Family Room

woman M.

Sequence

suite & pagoda

MAT()

guest suite

entry court

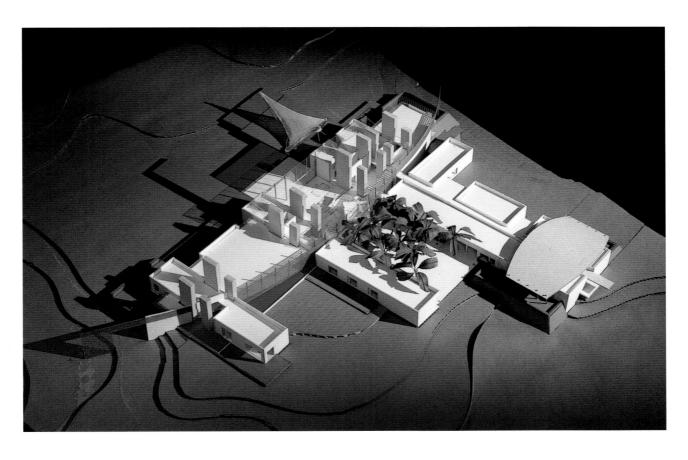

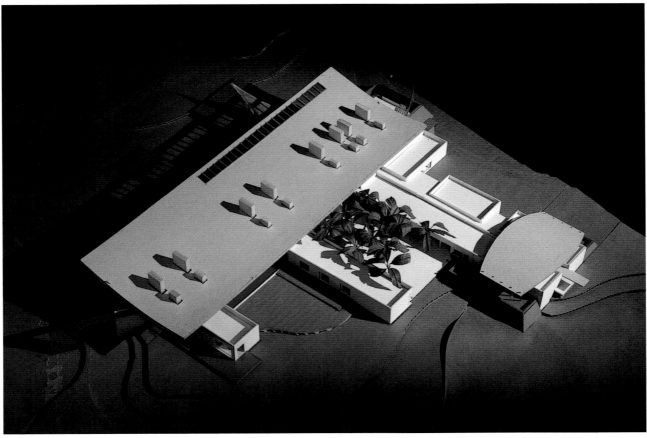

1. Steven Ehrlich, F.A.I.A., Principal
2. James Schmidt, A.I.A., Principal
3. Cecily Young, A.I.A., Principal
4. Thomas Zahlten, A.I.A., Principal
5. Alec Whitten
6. Mark Hansup Kim
7. George P. Elian
8. Whitney Wyatt

9. Justin Brechtel
10. Patricia Rhee
11. Ed Rolen
12. Tammee Taylor
13. Aaron Torrence
14. Haekwan Park
15. Janet Suen, AIA
16. Thomas Hanley

17. Robert Juarez
18. Magdalena Glen-Schieneman, AIA
19. Noreena Manio
20. Mathew Chaney
21. Mary Chou
22. Christina Monte
23. Natalie Torrence
24. George Cosmas

25. Nicole Pflug
26. Martijn Van Bentum
27. Leticia Balacek
28. Lee Lehnert
29. Luigi Imperatore

Alexia Zydel (not shown)

FIRM PROFILE

Steven Ehrlich Architects

Steven Ehrlich Architects is a thirty person architectural collective of gifted people whose atelier is a converted dance hall in Culver City, California. Ehrlich, who founded the firm in 1979 is now joined by three Principals: Cecily Young AIA, Thomas Zahlten AIA, and James Schmidt AIA, who has worked on many of the houses featured in this book.

The firm has been widely published and has won numerous design awards including three National AIA Awards in 1997. A Rizzoli monograph on Steven Ehrlich Architect's work was published in 1998 revealing the firm's contemporary designs that fuse technology with cultural and environmental sensitivity.

Current signature projects include: A 300,000-square-foot Medical research laboratory in Cambridge, Massachusetts for Lyme Properties. A new theatre complex for Center Theatre Group in Culver City, California, Art Centers for UCLA and Orange Coast College in Southern California, and master planning and five new campus buildings for San Bernardino Valley Community College. The Encino/Tarzana and Westwood libraries for the city of Los Angeles and residences which account for approximately half of the firm's work. Steven Ehrlich Architects designed DreamWork's 350,000-square-foot SKG Studio in Glendale, California, Sony Music Entertainment's 100,000-square-foot West Coast Headquarters in Santa Monica, California, and the Biblioteca Latino Americana in San Jose, California.

Steven Ehrlich, FAIA Design Principal

James Schmidt, AIA, Principal

BIOGRAPHIES

Steven Ehrlich, FAIA Design Principal

Steven Ehrlich learned early on the significance of how architecture responds to the culture and the environment. A self-proclaimed "architectural anthropologist," upon graduating from Rensselaer Polytechnic Institute in 1969, Ehrlich spent six years living and working in Africa, serving for two years with the Peace Corps as the first architect in Marrakech, Morocco. He later traveled across the Sahara and taught architecture at Ahmadu Bello University in Nigeria. The lessons of indigenous building have formed Ehrlich's approach to design and continue to influence his work today. Los Angeles, with its multi-cultural diversity, kinetic energy and open-minded nature, has proven fertile ground for his unique brand of Modernism. Within the artistic Los Angeles milieu, Steven has also championed the collaboration of artists and architects as well as fusing technology with cultural and environmental sensitivity. He has also taught at Montana State University, SCI-Arch, UCLA, and USC, as well as being a visiting design critic at Harvard, Yale and Woodbury. He has also lectured worldwide.

James Schmidt, AIA, Principal

Native to the Los Angeles basin, James studied architecture at California State University in San Luis Obispo, CA, as well as in Florence, Italy. James was drawn to Steven Ehrlich's work in 1990 for its modern vernacular language of residential projects. James collaborates with Steven on the residential commissions in the studio. The residences found in this book demonstrate James' careful attention to detail, space planning, patience with demanding client programs, understanding of difficult site restraints, and coordination of the consultant and architectural team.

DESIGN AWARDS

American Institute of Architects (AIA)

National AIA

2001 AIA/National American Library Association, **Robertson Branch Library**; Los Angeles, CA

1998 AIA/National Concrete Masonry Association, **Child Care Center**; Culver City, CA

1997 **Paul Cummins Library**, Crossroads School; Santa Monica, CA (Architecture)

1997 **Schulman Residence**; Brentwood, CA (Architecture)

1997 **Bow Truss Studios**, Sony Pictures Entertainment; Culver City, CA (Interiors)

1997 AIA/National American Library Association, **Paul Cummins Library**; Santa Monica, CA

1994 AIA/National Concrete Masonry Association, **Shatto Recreation Center**; Los Angeles, CA

California AIA

1998 **Paul Cummins Library**, Crossroads School; Santa Monica, CA; Merit Award

1996 **Child Care Center**; Culver City, CA; Merit Award

1995 **Farrell Residence**; Venice, CA; Honor Award

1995 **Schulman Residence**; Brentwood, CA; Merit Award

1991 **Israel Residence**; Santa Monica, CA; Honor Award

1990 **Windward Circle Redevelopment**; Venice, CA; Award of Merit

1987 **Ed Moses Studio**; Venice, CA; Commendation

1984 **Ahmadu Bello University Theater**; Zaria, Nigeria; Honor Award

1982 **Kalfus Studio**; Los Angeles, CA; Honor Award

Los Angeles AIA

1998 **Addition to Neutra Beach House**; Santa Monica, CA; Honor Award

1998 **Robertson Branch Library**, Los Angeles, CA; Distinguished Building Award

1997 **Paul Cummins Library**, Crossroads School; Santa Monica, CA; Merit Award

1997 **Child Care Center**; Culver City, CA; Merit Award

1996 **BUS Wellness Center**; Santa Monica, CA; Merit Award

1996 **Bow Truss Studios**, Sony Pictures Entertainment; Culver City, CA; Merit Award (Interiors)

1992 **Schulman Residence**; Los Angeles, CA; Honor Award

1992 **Shatto Recreation Center**; Los Angeles, CA; Honor Award

1989 **Okulick Studio**; Venice, CA; Award of Honor

1988 **Ed Moses Studio**; Venice, CA; Award of Merit

1983 **Swann Residence**; Santa Cruz, CA; Honor Award

1982 **Ahmadu Bello University Theater**; Zaria, Nigeria; Citation

1981 **Kalfus Studio**; Los Angeles, CA; Honor Award

International Awards

1995 **Taichung Civic Center Competition**; Taichung, Taiwan; Honorable Mention

National Awards

2002 Residential Architectural Design Awards, **Beach Lofts**; Venice, CA

1997 Boston Society of Architects, **Taichung City Civic Center**; City of Taichung, Taiwan

1996 Architectural Record, Record Interiors, **BUS Wellness Center**; Santa Monica, CA

1996 Custom Home Award, **Farrell Residence**; Venice, CA; Merit Award

1995 Builder's Choice Award, **Hempstead Residence**; Venice, CA; Grand Award

1994 Builder's Choice Award, **Sony Music Entertainment**; Santa Monica, CA

1992 Interior's Award, **Shatto Recreation Center**; Los Angeles, CA; Socially Conscious Award

1990 Builder's Choice Award, **Miller Residence**; Los Angeles, CA; Merit Award

1986 Builder's Choice Award, **Robertson Residence**; Santa Monica, CA; Merit Award

1985 Builder's Choice Award, **Kalfus Studio**; Los Angeles, CA; Grand Award

1983 Builder's Choice Award, **Swann Residence**; Santa Cruz, CA; Honorable Mention

Regional Awards

2001 San Jose AIA Design Awards, **Biblioteca**, San Jose, CA

2000 Design Award 2000, **Grand Central Arts Building**; California Preservation Foundation

1999 Ahwahnee Award, **Grand Central Arts Building**; Santa Ana, CA, Certificate of Merit

1999 San Diego AIA, **Grand Central Arts Building**; Santa Ana, CA

1997 San Diego AIA, Citation for Unbuilt Projects, **Grand Central Arts Building**; Santa Ana, CA

1997 Sunset/AIA Western Home Awards, **Farrell Residence**; Venice, CA; Merit Award

1996 Gold Nugget Award, **Bow Truss Studios**, Sony Pictures Entertainment; Grand Award

1995 Sunset/AIA Western Home Award, **Schulman Residence**; Brentwood, CA; Merit Award

1993 Gold Nugget Award, Project of the Year, **Sony Music Entertainment Campus**; Santa Monica, CA

1992 Concrete Masonry Award, **Shatto Recreation Center**; Los Angeles, CA; Grand Award

1992 Sunset AIA Interior Design Awards, **Gold-Friedman Residence**; Santa Monica, CA

1990 Western Red Cedar Lumber Association Design Awards, **Moses Studio**; Venice, CA; Merit Award

1988 Elan Award, **268 Townhouses**; Chatsworth, CA; Kaufman and Broad; Project of the Year

1983 Sunset AIA Award, **Kalfus Studio**; Los Angeles, CA; Award of Merit

Local Awards

2001 Los Angeles Business Council, **10865**; Los Angeles, CA

2001 Los Angeles Business Council, **Cnation**; Los Angeles, CA

1999 Westside Urban Forum Award, **Ten9Fifty**; Culver City, CA

1999 Los Angeles Business Council, **Addition to Neutra Beach House**, Los Angeles, CA

1998 Los Angeles Business Council, **Robertson Branch Library**; Los Angeles, CA

1997 LA Cultural Affairs Commission, **Robertson Branch Library**; Los Angeles, CA

1997 Los Angeles Business Council, **Paul Cummins Library**; Santa Monica, CA

1997 Los Angeles Business Council, **Bowtruss Studios/Gameshow Network**; Culver City, CA

1997 Los Angeles Business Council, **BUS Wellness Center**; Santa Monica, CA

1996 Los Angeles Business Council, **Child Care Center**; Culver City, CA

1996 Los Angeles Business Council, **Farrell Residence**; Venice, CA

1995 Los Angeles Business Council, **Hempstead Residence**; Venice, CA

1994 Los Angeles Business Council, **Sony Music Campus**; Santa Monica, CA

1994 Los Angeles Business Council, **Shatto Recreation Center**; Los Angeles, CA

1994 Los Angeles Business Council, **Schulman Residence**; Los Angeles, CA

1994 Los Angeles Business Council, **Aspect Ratio**; Los Angeles, CA

1989 Los Angeles Business Council, **Ehrlich Residence**; Santa Monica, CA

1989 LA Cultural Affairs Commission, **Shatto Recreation Center**; Los Angeles, CA

SELECTED BUILDINGS AND PROJECTS

NOTE: Bold—featured in book
Dates indicate completion

SINGLE FAMILY HOUSES

2004 **Dubai House, United Arab Emirates**

2003 Benarroch House, Los Angeles, California

2003 Leonard House, Los Angeles, California

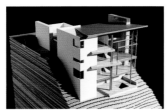

2003 **Ehrlich House, Venice, California**

2003 Goldstein-Porter House, Venice, California

2003 Boxenbaum House, Beverly Hills, **California**

2002 **Royer House, Venice, California**
2002 **Waldfogel House, Palo Alto, California**
2002 **Webster House, Venice, California**

2002 Koffler House, Pacific Palisades, California

2001 Wosk House (renovation), Santa Monica, California

2000 **Canyon House, Los Angeles, California**
1999 Lowe House, Los Angeles, California

1999 **Woods House (Renovation), Santa Monica, California**

1998 **Addition to Neutra Beach House, Santa Monica, California**

1998 Munitz House (renovation), Santa Monica, California

1997 Lo House, Diamond Bar, California

1997 Richards-Ebert House, Telluride, Colorado

1996 Hayashida House, Kobe, Japan

1996 Margolin House (renovation), Crestwood Hills, California

1995 Matchinger House (interior), Santa Barbara, California

1995 **Farrell House, Venice, California**

1994 Norred House, Malibu, California

1993 Israel House (Renovation), Brentwood, California

1993 Hempstead House, Venice, California

1992 Schulman House, Brentwood, California

1991 Douroux House, Venice, California
1991 Douroux Canal House, Venice, California
1991 Gold-Friedman House, Santa Monica, California

1991 Jenson House, Malibu, California
1990 Freidman House, Crestwood Hills, California
1990 Ehrman/Coombs House, Santa Monica, California
1990 Nesburn/Friedman House, Brentwood, California
1990 Chiate House, Malibu, California
1990 Plattner House, New Scotland, New York
1990 2311 Ocean Front House, Venice, California
1989 Ripple House, Venice, California
1988 Ehrlich House, Santa Monica, California
1987 Robertson House, Sun Valley, Idaho
1986 Miller-Nazarey House, Los Angeles, California

1986 Futiko-Tamagowon House of the Future, Tokyo, Japan (with Yamada & Associates)

1984 Vining-Doughty House, Lambertville, New Jersey
1984 Buchalter-Friedman House, Brentwood, California
1982 Semler House, Malibu, California
1981 Robertson House (renovation), Santa Monica, California
1979 Swann House, Scotts Valley, California
1974 Carey House, Grafton, Vermont
1974 Katz House, Dummerston, Vermont
1974 Taylor House, Westminster West, Vermont
1974 Rostane House, Okamiden, Morocco

MULTI-FAMILY RESIDENTIAL

2004 Center Street Housing for Lee Group, San Pedro, California
2003 San Pedro Tower Lofts for Lee Group San Pedro, California
2002 Beach Lofts—Venice, California
1991 Villa Del Este Condominiums, Corona del Mar, California
1989 California West Townhouses, Kaufman & Broad, Chatsworth, California
1985 Sundance Housing Development, Rialto, California
1972 Housing for New Rural Villages, Marrakech, Morocco

ARTIST STUDIOS/GALLERIES

2003 Orange Coast College, Art Gallery & Café, Costa Mesa, California
1989 Okulick Studio, Venice, California
1987 Moses Studio, Venice, California
1986 Dill Studio, Venice, California
1981 Kalfus Studio, Hollywood Hills, California

THEATRES

2005 Telluride Center for the Performing Arts, Telluride, Colorado
2003 The Culver Theater, Center Theatre Group, Culver City, California
1976 Ahmadu Bello University Theater, Zaria, Nigeria

LIBRARIES

2004 Westwood Branch Library, City of Los Angeles, California
2003 Encino-Tarzana Branch Library, City of Los Angeles, California
1999 Biblioteca Latinoamericana RDA, San Jose, California (with Garcia-Teague Architects + Interiors)
1997 Robertson Branch Library, Los Angeles, California
1997 Paul Cummins Library, Crossroads School, Santa Monica, California

RECREATION

1999 Washington United Youth Center RDA, San Jose, California (with Garcia-Teague)
1990 Shatto Recreation Center, Los Angeles, California

SCHOOLS & CAMPUSES

2004 Los Angeles Central Middle School #4, Los Angeles Unified School District, Los Angeles, California
2003 Los Angeles Community College Atwater Campus, Los Angeles, California
2003 San Bernardino Valley Community College, San Bernardino, California (with Thomas Blurock & Associates)
2002 Orange Coast College Art Center, Costa Mesa, California
2002 UCLA Southwest Staging Building, Los Angeles, California
1998 DreamWorks SKG Animation Studios, Glendale, California (with Gensler)
1994 Child Care Center, Sony Music Entertainment, Culver City, California
1992 Sony Music Entertainment West Coast Headquarters, Santa Monica, California

MIXED USE

2002 Kendall Square Medical/Biotech Laboratory, Lyme Properties, Cambridge, Massachusetts (with SMMA)
2000 Lantana East & South, for Hines, Santa Monica, California
1998 Ten9Fifty (Renovation), Culver City, California
1989 Ace Marketplace, Venice, California
1987 Windward Circle Arts Building, Venice, California
1988 Race Through the Clouds, Venice, California

ADAPTIVE REUSE

2001 Van De Kamp Bakery Building— Atwater District, Los Angeles, California
1998 Grand Central Arts Building, California State Fullerton, Santa Ana, California (with Robbins, Jergen, Christopher)
1998 10865 Washington Boulevard, Culver City, California
1994 Game Show Network, Sony Pictures Entertainment, Culver City, California

SELECTED BIBLIOGRAPHY

Books

Steven Ehrlich Architects Rizzoli
International Publications, Inc. New York
1998. Joseph Giovannini

Steven Ehrlich: Contemporary World
Architects Rockport Publishers, Rockport,
MA 1994. Eleanor Lynn Nesmith

Steven Ehrlich Architects - Casas CP 67.
Kliczkowski, Madrid/Buenos Aires 1998.
Oscar Riera Ojeda

Building A New Millennium Taschen,
Cologne, Germany 1999 (Addition to Neutra
Beach House)

Contemporary American Architects, Vol.I, IV
Taschen, Cologne, Germany 1995, 1998.
Philip Jodido

Contemporary California Architects, Vol. III
Taschen, Cologne, Germany 1997. Philip
Jodido

Modernism Reborn: Mid Century American
Houses Universe, New York 2001. Michael
Webb

The New American House 1 New York,
Whitney, 1995. Oscar Riera Ojeda
(Schulman House)

The New American House 3: Innovations in
Residential Design and Construction. 30 Case
Studies Whitney Library Design Publications.
New York, NY 2001. James Grayson Trulove
and Il Kim. (Canyon Residence)

Outdoor Rooms Gloucester, MA: Rockport
1998. Julie Taylor (Hempstead House)

Outside Architecture Gloucester, MA: Rizzoli
International Publications, Inc. New York
1998. Zevon, Susan. (Gold-Friedman House)

Stunning Houses Loft Publications,
Barcelona, Spain 1999

Interior Spaces of the USA and Canada
Volume 5 Melbourne, 2001

Periodicals

Abitare July/August 1999 Addition to Neutra
Beach House; April 1990 Windward Circle
Redevelopment

A+U #356 May 2000 Addition to Neutra
Beach House and Canyon Residence

AIA Journal December 1982 Kalfus Studio

Architecture May 1998 Robertson Branch
Library; September 1991 Shatto Recreation
Center; June 1987 Futiko– Tamagowan;

Architecture California January 1983 Kalfus
Studio; 1984 Ahmadu Bello University

Architectural Digest May 1996 Moses
Studio; August 1995 Farrell House; October
1993 Schulman Residence

Architectural Record November 2000 Kendall
Square; October 2000 Biblioteca
Latinoamericana; February 1999 Ten9Fifty;
August 1998 Addition to Neutra Beach
House; September 1996 Bus Wellness
Center; February 1995 GameShow Network

Architectural Review November 1998 Paul Cummins Library at Crossroads School; October 1998 Addition to Neutra Beach House; July 1994 Ehrman-Coombs House and Schulman Residence

DOMUS No. 667, December 1985 Robertson House and Swann House

GA Houses #71 Wosk Residence; #70 Ehrlich Residence; #62 Canyon Residence; #59 St. John Residence; #58 Woods Residence; #56 Addition to Neutra Beach House; #55 Canyon Residence; #49 Douroux House; #44 Farrell Residence; #39 Hempstead Residence, Schulman Residence & Ehrman-Coombs House; #21 Friedman House; #15 Kalfus Studio

Home Style October 2001 Canyon Residence

House Beautiful November 1998 Addition to Neutra Beach House

Interior Design November 1993 Sony Music Entertainment West Coast Headquarters

L.A. Architect September/October 2000 Biblioteca Latinoamericana; March/April 2000 Ten9Sixfive—Architects' Studio; April 1995 Child Care Center

L'ARCA June 1998 Robertson Branch Library; May 1997 Paul Cummins Library at Crossroads School; June 1997 Bus Wellness Center; April 1996 Child Care Center; September 1994 Schulman House; March 1994 Sony Music Entertainment West Coast Headquarters

Los Angeles Times February 27, 1999 Grand Central Arts Building; July 7, 1997 Robertson Branch Library; September 22, 1996 DreamWorks SKG Animation Studios; March 27, 1994 Hempstead House; September 13, 1992 Gold–Friedman House; March 15, 1992 Shatto Recreation Center; February 7, 1988 Moses Studio; December 13, 1981 Kalfus Studio

Metropolis October 1995 Child Care Center

Metropolitan Home November/December 2000 Woods Residence; May/June 1998 Lo House; May/June 1994 Hempstead House; September 1982 Kalfus Studio

Newsweek October 5, 1992 Shatto Recreation Center

The New York Times February 2002 Beach Lofts, Venice, California; June 18, 1998 Addition to Neutra Beach House; April 8, 1982 Kalfus Studio

Orange County Register February 2002 Orange Coast College, Orange Coast, California

Towne & Country August 1999 Addition to Neutra Beach House

Wall Street Journal December 13,1996 Schulman Residence

ACKNOWLEDGMENTS

First and foremost, I wish to thank all of my clients whose houses are represented in this book. They all took a giant leap of faith when they asked me to collaborate with them on creating their homes, and I appreciate their trust.

I must thank my superb, dedicated team at Steven Ehrlich Architects, beginning with principal James Schmidt, AIA, my collaborator on residential projects since 1990. I also wish to acknowledge principals Cecily Young, AIA, and Thomas Zahlten, AIA, along with architectural team members Alec Whitten, Thomas Hanley, Justin Brechtel, George Elian, Matthew Chaney and Ed Rolen for their important contributions to these projects. Thanks also go to all of our skilled model builders. I also thank previous staff member M. Charles Bernstein for his special contributions to the Shulman Residence along with Gary Alzona, John Girard and Mary Kim. Thanks as well to our support staff, especially Tammee Taylor and also to Christina Monti and Natalie Torrence.

I am indebted to the contractors who made these houses stand up and shine, including Mark Shramek, Winters-Schram, Don Latinshlager, Sanchez Brothers, Elliot Prather and Ken Royer.

My admiration and appreciation goes to Michael Webb, for his thoughtful, insightful and illuminating text; also to all of the photographers who have so skillfully captured the essence of form and space: Tom Bonner, Grey Crawford, Dennis Freppel, Melba Levick, Edward Linden, Thomas Loof, Lawrence Manning, Julius Shulman/David Glomb, Tim Street-Porter, and Alan Weintraub; thanks as well to ace computer 3-D imagists Craig Shimahara and Cameron Crockett.

Finally and not least, I am deeply grateful to my publishers Paul Latham and Alessina Brooks at The Images Publishing Group. They and their team worked tirelessly to put this book together, and I wish to extend special thanks to designer Rod Gilbert, who is a pleasure to work with, and to Images coordinator Jodie Davis.

IMAGE CREDITS

Photographers

Alia: 118
Tom Bonner: 22; 55 (top right); 55 (bottom); 75; 76–77; 80; 82; 84; 85; 115
Greg Cloud: 55 (models)
Grey Crawford: 122 (Lowe, Hempsted); 123 (Gold-Friedman)
Christopher Dow: 123 (Miller)
East West Photo Color Inc.: 123 (Futiko Tamagowan)
Dennis Freppel: 101; 104; 105; 106–107; 109; 111; 122 (Leonard and Boxenbaum)
Melba Levick: 122 (Wosk)
John Linden: 55 (top left); 56; 66–72
Thomas Loof: Cover; 6; 88–89; 92–93; 94–99
Lawrence Manning: 12; 13; 16; 50–53; 118 (right)
Luckman Studios/UCLA Archive: 54
Julius Shulman/David Glomb: 3; 57
Tim Street-Porter: 61–65
Alan Weintraub: 23–28; 81; 83

Computer Images

Craig Shimahara: 13; 15; 18–21; 31–33; 36–37; 39; 42–43; 45–47
Cameron Crocket: 86 (right); 87

Digital Plans/Sections

Justin Brechtel
Edward Rolen

Freehand Sketches

Steven Ehrlich

128

The information and illustrations have been
prepared and supplied by Steven Ehrlich and
Michael Webb. While all efforts have been made
to source the required information and ensure
accuracy, the publishers do not, under any
circumstances, accept responsibility for errors,
omissions and representations express or implied.